Beef

GENERAL EDITOR
CHUCK WILLIAMS

RECIPES
JOYCE GOLDSTEIN

PHOTOGRAPHY
ALLAN ROSENBERG

TIME
LIFE
BOOKS

Time-Life Books
is a division of TIME LIFE INC.,
a wholly owned subsidiary of
THE TIME INC. BOOK COMPANY

President: John M. Fahey

TIME-LIFE BOOKS
President: John Hall
Vice President and Publisher, Custom Publishing:
   Susan J. Maruyama
Director of Custom Publishing: Frances C. Mangan
Director of Marketing: Nancy K. Jones

WILLIAMS-SONOMA
Founder/Vice-Chairman: Chuck Williams

WELDON OWEN INC.
President: John Owen
Publisher: Wendely Harvey
Managing Editor: Laurie Wertz
Consulting Editor: Norman Kolpas
Copy Editor: Sharon Silva
Editorial Assistant: Janique Poncelet
Design: John Bull, The Book Design Company
Production: Stephanie Sherman, Mick Bagnato
Food Photographer: Allan Rosenberg
Associate Food Photographer: Allen V. Lott
Primary Food & Prop Stylist: Sandra Griswold
Food Stylist: Heidi Gintner
Assistant Food Stylist: Danielle Di Salvo
Prop Assistant: Karen Nicks
Glossary Illustrations: Alice Harth

The Williams-Sonoma Kitchen Library
conceived and produced by Weldon Owen Inc.
814 Montgomery St., San Francisco, CA 94133

In collaboration with Williams-Sonoma
100 North Point, San Francisco, CA 94133

Production by Mandarin Offset, Hong Kong
Printed in China

A Note on Weights and Measures:
All recipes include customary U.S., U.K. and
metric measurements. Conversions are based on
a standard developed for these books and have
been rounded off. Actual weights may vary.

A Weldon Owen Production

Copyright © 1993 Weldon Owen Inc.

Library of Congress
Cataloging-in-Publication Data:

Goldstein, Joyce Esersky.
   Beef / general editor, Chuck Williams ;
recipes, Joyce Goldstein ; photography,
Allan Rosenberg.
      p.   cm. — (Williams-Sonoma
      kitchen library)
   Includes index.
   ISBN 0-7835-0245-1 (trade) ;
   ISBN 0-7835-0246-X (library)
   1. Cookery (Beef)   I. Williams, Chuck.
II. Title.   III. Series.
TX749.5.B43G64   1993
641.6'62—dc20   93-17989
                                           CIP

Contents

BRAISED & STEWED 17

SAUTÉED 51

BROILED & GRILLED 77

ROASTED & BAKED 95

INTRODUCTION

Down through the ages, beef has been virtually synonymous with eating well. From the humblest of hamburgers and stews to the most glorious of standing rib roasts, a main course of meat can make any meal seem like a feast.

Yet many of today's cooks, faced with new findings on the links between diet and health, have turned away from beef, despite the fact that it remains an outstanding source of nutrients. In response, the meat industry has developed new strains of cattle and new feeding methods to produce leaner beef without sacrificing flavor or tenderness.

In like-minded spirit, this book aims to restore beef to its rightful place on the dining table. It begins with an overview of the simple kitchen equipment you'll need to prepare it, as well as a guide to buying and storing beef and veal. Step-by-step photographs cover the basics of stock making and the various cooking methods. Also included are a few recipes for sauces and seasoned butters that can be used to dress up simple roasts and steaks.

Following these fundamentals are 44 easily prepared recipes for a wide repertoire of beef and veal dishes, organized into chapters on braising and stewing, sautéing, broiling and grilling, and roasting and baking. A full-color photograph accompanies each recipe, to provide both inspiration and guidance. As you look through the book, you'll note that many of the dishes employ the leaner, more reasonably priced cuts that have been finding so much favor among nutritionists and health-conscious cooks alike.

I hope these recipes will entice you into the kitchen to prepare your own home-cooked meal featuring beef.

Chuck Williams

EQUIPMENT

*All-purpose cookware, plus a few specialized tools,
will produce a wide range of beef and veal dishes*

A relatively few pieces of equipment, many of them
already in the average kitchen, will meet the needs of
most beef and veal recipes. Good-quality knives with
sharp blades and well-attached handles, for example,
serve many purposes; so do such cooking vessels
as a stockpot, sauté and frying pans, saucepan,
casserole and roasting pan.

   Among the several specialized utensils
shown here, an instant-read thermometer
comes particularly recommended. Inserted into
a roast when it has spent the minimum estimated
cooking time in the oven, it provides a quick and
accurate reading of internal temperature—the
surest gauge of doneness.

1. Stockpot
Tall, deep, large-capacity pot
with close-fitting lid, for
making stock or boiling or
braising large cuts of beef.
Select a good-quality heavy pot
that absorbs and transfers heat
well. Anodized aluminum,
shown here, or enameled steel
cleans easily and does not react
with the acidity of any wine,
citrus juice or tomatoes added
during cooking.

2. Strainer
For straining solids from stock.

3. Saucepan
For simmering sauces for roast,
broiled (grilled) or panfried
beef.

4. Meat Pounder
Heavy stainless-steel disk with
sturdy handle, used to flatten
veal scallops for quick cooking

or slices of beef to be rolled
and stuffed.

5. Skimmer
Wide bowl and fine mesh for
efficient removal of froth and
scum from surface of beef stock.

6. Roasting Pan and Rack
Heavy, durable metal pan large
enough to hold beef roasts.
Sturdy, stick-resistant metal
rack facilitates lifting and

turning, promotes even
roasting and prevents roasts
from sticking to pan.

7. Vegetable Peeler
Curved, slotted swiveling blade
thinly strips away the peel from
root vegetables to be added to
stews and braises.

8. Paring Knife
For peeling vegetables and
cutting up small ingredients.

9. Carving Fork
Sturdy two-pronged fork
steadies roasts during carving.

10. Carving Knife
Long, sturdy-but-flexible blade
easily slices through large cuts
of beef.

11. Chef's Knife
All-purpose knife for chopping
and slicing large items or large
quantities of ingredients.

iron or enamel for rapid browning or frying. Sloped, shallow sides facilitate turning of meat and allow moisture to escape more easily for crispier, better-browned results.

17. Pot Holder
Heavy-duty cotton provides good protection from hot cookware.

18. Sauté Pan
For good browning in the early stages of sautéing, select a well-made heavy metal pan large enough to hold pieces of meat in a single layer without crowding. Straight sides about 2½ inches (6 cm) high help contain splattering. Close-fitting lid covers pan during moist-cooking stage.

19. Meat Thermometer
Standard meat thermometer, inserted into the thickest part of a roast before it goes into the oven.

20. Wooden Toothpicks
Used to secure slices of meat rolled or folded around a stuffing for braising.

21. Kitchen String
For tying stuffed and rolled slices of meat or holding larger cuts together in compact shapes for even cooking. Choose good-quality linen string, which withstands intense heat with minimal charring.

22. Wooden Skewers
For holding together small pieces of meat during broiling or grilling. Before using, soak in water for 30 minutes to prevent burning.

12. Sharpening Steel
Used regularly, large, rod-shaped steel sharpening tool keeps kitchen blades finely honed.

13. Casserole
For use on the stove top or in the oven, large-capacity enameled metal cooking vessel with tight-fitting ovenproof lid holds baked foods, braises and stews.

14. Assorted Kitchen Tools
Crockery jar holds metal spatula for turning hamburgers and other panfried foods; rubber spatula for mixing stuffings; slotted spoon for stirring stews and braises; tongs for turning meats on the grill or under the broiler (griller); wire whisks and wooden spoons for stirring sauces; basting brush for moistening meats on the grill; bulb baster for basting roasts; and an instant-read thermometer for testing meat for doneness.

15. Cheesecloth
Used in double thickness to line strainers and filter out fine particles when straining stock. Muslin can also be used.

16. Frying Pan
Choose good-quality, heavy aluminum, stainless steel, cast

Beef Basics

Guidelines to help you select the right cut and best quality for any recipe

A major source of protein, iron, phosphorous, zinc and five B-complex vitamins, beef is indisputably nutritious. Yet, in recent years, more attention has been paid to its saturated fat and cholesterol content, with its merits often ignored.

The meat industry has responded dramatically to consumers' needs, offering beef that can play a part in heart-healthy diets. Cattle growers now breed leaner animals; butchers trim away more visible fat. A 3-ounce (90-g) portion of cooked, trimmed lean beef today has only 8.4 grams of fat and just 73 milligrams of cholesterol, well within the daily dietary recommendation of 300 milligrams.

A cut's leanness ultimately depends, however, upon which part of the animal it comes from. Cuts from more active muscles—chuck and round, for instance—are naturally tougher and leaner than lightly used muscle sections like rib and short loin. Tougher, leaner cuts are best cooked by moist methods such as braising or stewing; more tender cuts do better with dry methods like grilling, broiling or roasting. (For guides to the beef and veal cuts used in this book, see the glossary.)

Guidelines for Buying Quality Beef and Veal

Government inspectors in the United States classify beef into eight categories, the three highest of which are Prime (the best), Choice and Select. Prime beef is found in limited quantities, in restaurants and some top-quality meat markets. Choice and Select are the most common grades available at food markets. In grading, primary consideration is given to the degree of marbling, which is the distribution of flecks of white fat. This fat produces more tender and flavorful meat. The age of the animal, the color, texture and marbling of the meat, and how long the meat has been aged are also defining characteristics.

Prime beef, with the most marbling, is also the highest in fat; Choice and Select cuts are progressively leaner and therefore more healthful. Excess fat should be trimmed off in any case. Whatever cut and grade you buy, look for meat that is bright cherry red. Vacuum-packaged meat may appear more purplish; its color will brighten on exposure to air.

Veal, the meat of three- to five-month-old calves, is prized for its pale color, mild flavor, tender texture and leanness. Good-quality veal is fine-grained and creamy pink, with any visible fat a pure milky white.

Storing Beef and Veal

As soon as you return home, put beef or veal in the coldest part of the refrigerator, loosening the wrapping to provide air circulation. Use uncooked whole cuts of beef or leftover cooked beef within 3 to 4 days, and uncooked veal or ground (minced) beef in 1 to 2 days.

You can freeze meat for up to 2 weeks in its retail package. For longer freezing of up to 6 months, wrap securely in polyethylene film, heavy-duty aluminum foil or freezer paper; label and date the package.

Defrost in the refrigerator, allowing 4 to 7 hours per pound (500 g) for large cuts, 3 to 5 hours per pound for smaller cuts; or use a microwave oven, following manufacturer's directions.

Oriental Roast Beef

Beef Stock

Making a good stock at home is an all-day task, but the results are well worth the time. Prepare a large batch and freeze in small containers for future use. Beef stock keeps well in a tightly closed container in the refrigerator for about 5 days, or in the freezer for up to 6 months. If, however, you don't have time to make stock, you may substitute canned beef broth, which tends to be salty; taste the finished dish before adding any salt.

1. Browning the beef shanks.
Place meaty pieces of beef shank in a roasting pan and roast in a 450°F (220°C) oven until browned. Transfer to a large stockpot (shown above) and add cold water to cover.

2. Skimming and simmering.
Bring to a boil, regularly skimming off any scum or froth with a skimmer. Add aromatic vegetables, browned in the roasting pan, and herbs; simmer for at least 8 hours.

6 lb (3 kg) meaty beef shanks (shins)
beef scraps or other trimmings, if available
2 onions, coarsely chopped
1 leek, trimmed, carefully washed and coarsely chopped
2 carrots, peeled and coarsely chopped
1 celery stalk, coarsely chopped
mushroom stems, optional
6 cloves garlic
4 fresh parsley sprigs
10 whole peppercorns
3 fresh thyme sprigs
2 small bay leaves

*P*reheat an oven to 450°F (220°C). Place the beef shanks in a large roasting pan and put into the oven. Roast, turning occasionally, until browned but not burned, about 1½ hours.

Transfer the browned shanks to a large stockpot, reserving the juices in the pan, and add cold water to cover. Add any beef scraps you have on hand. Bring to a boil and skim off any scum and froth on the surface. Reduce the heat and simmer, uncovered, for 2 hours. Add water as needed to keep the bones generously immersed and skim the scum from the surface occasionally.

Meanwhile, place the roasting pan on the stove top. Add the onions, leek, carrots and celery to the fat remaining in the pan. Brown over high heat, stirring often, until the vegetables caramelize but are not scorched, 15–20 minutes. When the shanks have simmered for 2 hours, add the browned vegetables to the stockpot. Pour 1 cup (8 fl oz/250 ml) hot water into the roasting pan, bring to a simmer and deglaze the pan by stirring to dislodge any browned bits. Add these juices to the pot.

Place the mushroom stems, if using, garlic, parsley, peppercorns, thyme and bay leaves on a square of cheesecloth (muslin) and tie into a small bag with kitchen string. Add to the stockpot. Simmer, uncovered, over low heat, for 6 hours longer (for a total of 8 hours), or preferably the whole day.

Remove from the heat and remove the solids with a slotted spoon or skimmer. Pour the stock through a strainer. Line the strainer with cheesecloth and strain the stock again. Refrigerate, uncovered, until cool, then cover tightly.

For a richer stock, boil the strained stock, uncovered, until reduced by half or more. Refrigerate as directed above.

Before using stock, remove the fat that solidifies on the top.

Makes 4–5 qt (4–5 l)

Braising & Stewing

Two simple, related methods for simmering tough cuts of beef or veal to tenderness

Both classified as moist methods of cooking, braising and stewing have in common the fact that they employ some form of flavored liquid such as stock or wine as the cooking medium. In braising, larger pieces of meat are cooked in a small amount of liquid that usually forms a sauce. Stewing, on the other hand, cooks smaller, often bite-sized pieces of meat with proportionately more liquid, which becomes an integral part of the finished dish.

Because both braising and stewing impart moistness and promote tenderness through long, gentle simmering, they are ideally suited to tougher, leaner cuts of beef and veal from the leg, shoulder or neck sections such as brisket, round (rump) or chuck. But other cuts, too, may be cooked by these methods, particularly when the subtle mingling of flavors that results is desired, as in the Sicilian stuffed steak rolls on page 21 or the stuffed cabbage on page 27.

Braising and stewing share a few basic steps. First, the meat may be browned in some fat or oil to seal in its juices and intensify its color and taste. Use a wide, shallow sauté pan and do not crowd the meat; the steam must escape easily so it does not interfere with the browning process.

The browned meat is transferred to a large, heavy pot in which aromatic vegetables have been gently sautéed. Then, the cooking liquid is added—sometimes along with the deglazed deposits from the pan in which the meat was browned (see box, opposite)—and brought to a boil. The heat is reduced and the braise or stew is gently simmered until the meat is absolutely tender.

Greek Beef Stew

1. Browning the meat.
Heat fat or oil in a large, heavy sauté pan or frying pan over high heat. Add the meat, in batches if necessary to avoid overcrowding the pan; brown well on all sides, turning with metal tongs or a fork.

2. Sautéing aromatic vegetables.
In a large, heavy pot over medium heat, warm more fat or oil and sauté any aromatic vegetables—here, onions—until tender.

3. Adding the cooking liquid.
Add the browned meat to the pot and pour in the cooking liquid—here, beef stock. Add seasonings and other ingredients, bring to a boil, then lower the heat and simmer gently, covered, until the meat is tender, 1 hour or more.

SAUTÉING

Rapidly cooking tender pieces of meat, complete with garnishes and sauce

Named from the French verb *sauter*, "to jump," sautéing refers to turning or tossing quick-cooking ingredients—such as thin strips of beef fillet, veal scallops or ground (minced) beef patties—in a little hot fat or oil. Then, accompanying ingredients may be added along with a liquid to deglaze the pan and complete the cooking. Below are representative sautéing steps—in this case, veal scallops.

1. Pounding a veal scallop.
To help the meat sauté quickly and evenly, place it between 2 sheets of plastic wrap and pound gently with a meat pounder to a uniform ¼-inch (6-mm) thickness.

2. Browning the veal.
Heat butter and/or oil in a large sauté pan or frying pan. Add the veal, in batches if necessary, and sauté until golden, 2–3 minutes per side, turning it once with a spatula or tongs.

3. Deglazing the pan.
To dissolve the savory glaze of meat juices left in the pan, add a flavorful liquid—here, veal stock—and stir and scrape with a wooden spoon. Spoon the liquid over the meat, or use it as part of a simple sauce.

BROILING & GRILLING

Dry-heat cooking for tender cuts of beef and veal

The main secret to success in broiling and grilling beef is to buy the highest-quality meat and the most appropriate cut for these methods of dry cooking. Fillets are the mildest of the tender cuts, with the least fat, and when broiled or grilled may be nicely highlighted by a flavored butter (page 15) or sauce. Well-marbled sirloin steaks, New York strips or rib eyes and veal chops need just salt and pepper to bring out their flavor. Flank and skirt steaks, being chewier, require marinating to achieve maximum flavor and tenderness.

Whether you cook the steaks under a broiler (griller) or on an outdoor or indoor grill, preheating is essential. Cook the meat 4–6 inches (10–15 cm) from the heat. Cooking times will vary with the intensity of the heat and the thickness of the meat and its distance from the heat. For maximum juiciness and tenderness, steak is usually served rare (about 3 minutes per side; 125°F/52°C on an instant-read thermometer inserted into the center) to medium-rare (4 minutes; 130°F/54°C). Veal chops are also commonly served rare to medium-rare. Or try testing for doneness as professional chefs do, by touching the meat. Rare feels soft to the touch; medium is moderately firm.

Roasting Beef & Veal

Cooking in an oven's dry heat to intensify flavor

Cooked in the dry heat of an oven, large, tender cuts of beef or veal such as rib, rump, sirloin, round or chuck, or loaves of ground (minced) meat, develop nicely browned surfaces while staying moist and flavorful within.

A moderate oven temperature of 350°F (180°C) produces juicy roast beef with minimal shrinkage, but a higher temperature may be called for in some recipes to develop a richer crust. For veal, roast at a lower constant temperature of 325°F (165°C). Throughout roasting, baste the meat at regular intervals with its pan juices, its marinade or some other liquid such as wine or stock.

It is hard to give an accurate roasting timetable. Leaner cuts, for example, cook faster, and a roast's shape may affect its cooking time. The best way to ensure the desired degree of doneness is with an accurate meat thermometer—whether the kind inserted into the thickest part of the meat before it enters the oven, or an instant-read thermometer inserted at the earliest moment the roast may be done to your liking. The latter is generally preferred for its accuracy.

Check the meat with a thermometer the moment it is removed from the oven. Internal temperatures for varying degrees of doneness are as follows: 115°F (46°C) for very rare, 120°F (49°C) for rare, 125°F (52°C) for medium-rare, 135°F (57°C) for medium and 145°F (63°C) for well. Left standing at room temperature for 15–20 minutes, the roast will continue to cook inside and the internal temperature will increase 5°–8°F (2°–3°C). Its juices will also settle, making for easier carving.

Corresponding roasting times are 12 minutes per pound (500 g) for very rare, 13 minutes for rare, 14 minutes for medium-rare, 15 minutes for medium and 18 minutes for well-done. Cook veal roasts until medium to well-done. Boneless roasts cook more quickly than those with bones. These times will also vary according to the size and shape of the meat and are best used as general guidelines for when to check temperature.

The boneless prime rib of beef shown above (recipe, page 97) was rolled and tied by the butcher for more even cooking. To impart greater flavor to the meat, garlic slivers were inserted into slits in the roast at least 1 hour ahead, and its surface was seasoned with soy sauce, pepper and allspice. The meat was roasted—and basted at 10-minute intervals with dark beer—until its internal temperature read 125°–130°F (52°–54°C) on a meat thermometer. It was then left to stand for 15 minutes before being carved across the grain into slices ¼–½ inch (6–12 mm) thick with a sharp knife.

Mustard Cream Sauce

Here is a creamy sauce that complements roast beef, sautéed fillet of beef or broiled veal chops. It is also delectable with sautéed or roast chicken, roast pork loin, and poached or broiled salmon. The sauce is rich but tangy and provides a nice accent to a host of vegetables as well, including beets, carrots, green beans or simple boiled potatoes. It can be prepared a few hours in advance and reheated gently over low heat. Tarragon and chives have a natural affinity for mustard-based sauces and either one can be added at the last minute or two.

2 tablespoons unsalted butter
2 tablespoons all-purpose (plain) flour
1 cup (8 fl oz/250 ml) chicken stock, heated
5–6 tablespoons (3 oz/90 g) Dijon mustard
1 cup (8 fl oz/250 ml) heavy (double) cream
2 tablespoons chopped fresh tarragon, optional
2 tablespoons chopped fresh chives, optional
salt and freshly ground pepper

Melt the butter in a saucepan over medium heat. Add the flour and cook, stirring, a few minutes. Gradually add the stock, whisking constantly. Whisk in the mustard and cream and simmer until slightly thickened, about 5 minutes. Stir in the herbs, if using, and season to taste with salt and pepper. Serve hot.

Makes about 2 cups
(16 fl oz/500 ml)

Cold Horseradish Cream

Ideal for serving with boiled beef (recipe on page 28), hot or cold, as well as cold rare roast beef, broiled steak or boiled tongue (page 45, without the sweet-sour sauce). This sauce can be warmed gently over low heat and spooned over hot rib-eye or fillet steaks. Great on cooked salmon, too. You may use 5 tablespoons (3 oz/90 g) prepared horseradish for making this sauce, but the fresh root is hotter and better. If you use prepared horseradish, you may not need as much vinegar or salt.

½ cup (4 oz/125 g) thinly sliced, peeled fresh
  horseradish
3–4 tablespoons (about 2 fl oz/60 ml) distilled white
  vinegar
3 tablespoons finely minced white onion
1½ cups (12 fl oz/375 ml) sour cream
½ cup (4 fl oz/125 ml) heavy (double) cream
1 teaspoon salt
½ teaspoon freshly ground pepper
3 tablespoons chopped fresh dill or chives, optional

Place the horseradish and 3 tablespoons vinegar in a food processor fitted with the metal blade or in a blender. Purée until smooth. Transfer to a bowl. Stir in the remaining ingredients until well mixed, adding another tablespoon vinegar if needed for tartness and flavor balance.

Makes about 2 cups
(16 fl oz/500 ml)

Cold Horseradish Cream

Mustard Cream Sauce

13

Basic Tomato Sauce

Tomato sauce is an invaluable addition to the basic pantry. It can be used not only in a variety of beef dishes, such as veal alla parmigiana (recipe on page 52), but also to dress a simple pasta and to enrich soups, sauces or stews. As fresh tomatoes vary dramatically in quality and flavor, for the most consistent year-round sauce, use canned plum tomatoes, preferably those prepared in the Italian style, which usually come packed in tomato purée. Adding more canned tomato purée assures you of a thick sauce with excellent coating properties. This can be stored in a tightly covered container in the refrigerator for about 1 week. Add chopped fresh herbs at serving time, if you like.

2 cans (28 oz/875 g each) plum (Roma) tomatoes
1 cup (8 fl oz/250 ml) canned tomato purée
3 tablespoons unsalted butter or olive oil
salt and freshly ground pepper

Place the tomatoes with some of their juices in a food processor fitted with the metal blade and process until finely chopped but neither puréed nor too chunky. Transfer to a heavy, nonreactive saucepan.

Place over low heat and stir in the tomato purée. Cook, stirring often, until the sauce thickens slightly, about 10 minutes. Stir in the butter or oil and season to taste with salt and pepper.

Makes about 6 cups (48 fl oz/1.5 l)

Caper Sauce

This sauce is good on plain boiled beef (recipe on page 28), tongue (page 45, without the sauce) or cold roast beef. It also is excellent on cooked fish and steamed vegetables such as potatoes, carrots, beets or green beans. For a less tart taste, use fresh lemon juice to replace some of the vinegar. The optional bread crumbs add thickness and body to the sauce.

1 cup (1½ oz/45 g) chopped fresh parsley
⅓ cup (1½ oz/45 g) drained capers, coarsely chopped
½ cup (2½ oz/75 g) finely minced white onion
⅓ cup (3 fl oz/80 ml) wine vinegar
1¼ cups (10 fl oz/310 ml) olive oil
1–2 tablespoons finely minced, drained anchovy fillets
  in olive oil
2–4 cornichons, finely minced, optional
½ cup (2 oz/60 g) fine dried bread crumbs, optional
salt and freshly ground pepper

In a bowl stir together all the ingredients, including salt and pepper to taste, until well mixed.

Makes about 2½ cups (20 fl oz/625 ml)

Caper Sauce

Basic Tomato Sauce

Flavored Butters

These flavorful toppings, also known as composed or compound butters, melt into smooth, rich sauces when placed on broiled or grilled steaks, chops and burgers. Store the butters in tightly covered bowls. Or shape them into logs and wrap in plastic, then refrigerate and slice into rounds for serving. They will keep for up to 4 days in the refrigerator or for about 1 month in the freezer. Bring to room temperature before serving.

ROQUEFORT BUTTER

Delicious on steaks, veal chops and tucked into hamburgers.

3 oz (90 g) Roquefort cheese
6 tablespoons (3 oz/90 g) unsalted butter, at room temperature
2 tablespoons Cognac
1 teaspooon freshly ground pepper
¼ cup (1 oz/30 g) chopped walnuts, optional

Place the cheese, butter, Cognac and pepper in a food processor fitted with the metal blade. Process thoroughly. Alternatively, place in a blender and blend until smooth, or place in a bowl and beat with a whisk or an electric mixer until smooth. Transfer to a bowl and fold in the walnuts, if using.
Makes about ¾ cup (6 oz/180 g)

PROVENÇAL OLIVE BUTTER

Steaks and veal chops are wonderful served with this butter. It is also tasty spread on toast, tucked under the skin of chicken before broiling, swirled into pasta, or spooned over cooked vegetables such as tomatoes, beets, green beans, potatoes, fennel or carrots.

1 cup (5 oz/155 g) green or black olives, pitted
grated zest of 1 orange
2 tablespoons Cognac
2 shallots, finely minced
2 teaspoons finely minced fresh thyme
1 teaspoon finely minced garlic
1 tablespoon finely minced, drained anchovy fillets in olive oil
¾ cup (6 oz/180 g) unsalted butter, at room temperature
freshly ground pepper

Place the olives in a food processor fitted with the metal blade or in a blender and pulse just to chop. Add the orange zest, Cognac, shallots, thyme, garlic and anchovy and pulse just to combine. Add the butter and process until combined but still lightly textured. Season to taste with pepper.
Makes about 1½ cups (12 oz/375 g)

MUSTARD-CHIVE BUTTER

This is great on steaks or veal chops, as well as broiled chicken or poached salmon.

1 tablespoon dry mustard
½ teaspoon sugar
2 tablespoons distilled white vinegar or water
¼ cup (2 oz/60 g) Dijon mustard
½ cup (4 oz/125 g) plus 2 tablespoons unsalted butter, at room temperature
¼ cup (1½ oz/45 g) minced fresh chives
salt and freshly ground pepper

In a small bowl dissolve the dry mustard and sugar in the vinegar or water. Stir in the Dijon mustard. Transfer to a food processor fitted with the metal blade and add the butter and chives. Process to blend thoroughly. Alternatively, place in a blender and blend until smooth, or place in a bowl and beat with a whisk or an electric mixer until smooth. Season to taste with salt and pepper.
Makes about ⅔ cup (5 oz/155 g)

Beef Bourguignon

½ lb (250 g) salt pork, cut into ¼-inch
  (6-mm) dice

olive oil as needed

8 shallots, finely diced

2 onions, diced

2 carrots, peeled and diced

2 cloves garlic, minced

about 2 cups (8 oz/250 g) all-purpose
  (plain) flour

salt, freshly ground pepper and freshly
  grated nutmeg

3 lb (1.5 kg) well-marbled stewing beef,
  cut into 2-inch (5-cm) cubes

¼ cup (2 fl oz/60 ml) Cognac

2 cups (16 fl oz/500 ml) beef stock
  (preferably homemade, see page 9)

2 fresh thyme sprigs

3 cups (24 fl oz/750 ml) dry red wine

1 bay leaf

18–24 pearl onions, unpeeled

5 tablespoons (2½ oz/80 g) unsalted
  butter

2 tablespoons sugar

1 lb (500 g) fresh mushrooms, stemmed

chopped fresh parsley for garnish

In a frying pan over medium heat, fry the salt pork to render (melt) the fat, 8–10 minutes. Using a slotted spoon, transfer the pork bits to paper towels to drain; set aside. Add enough oil to the fat in the pan to measure ¼ cup (2 fl oz/60 ml) in all. Add the shallots, diced onions, carrots and garlic. Sauté until the vegetables are slightly soft, about 10 minutes; using a slotted spoon transfer to a large, heavy pot.

Mix the flour and salt, pepper and nutmeg to taste on a plate and use to coat the beef. Over high heat add oil as needed to the fat in the pan and brown the beef well, about 15 minutes. Using a slotted spoon, transfer the beef to the large pot. Add the Cognac and a little of the beef stock to the frying pan and deglaze over high heat, stirring to dislodge any browned bits. Add to the beef along with the thyme, all but ½ cup (4 fl oz/125 ml) of the stock, the wine and bay leaf. Bring to a boil, reduce the heat, cover and simmer on the stove or in an oven preheated to 325°F (165°C) until the beef is tender, about 3 hours.

Meanwhile, peel the pearl onions as directed in the glossary (see page 106). Warm 2 tablespoons of the butter in a sauté pan over medium heat. Add the onions in a single layer and sprinkle with the sugar. Cook, stirring, until tender and golden, 8–10 minutes; add only enough of the remaining stock to prevent scorching. Transfer to a bowl; set aside.

Warm the remaining 3 tablespoons butter in the same pan over medium heat. Add the mushrooms and brown on both sides, a few minutes; set aside.

During the last 30 minutes of cooking, add the mushrooms and onions to the beef. Adjust the seasoning. Sprinkle with the salt pork bits and parsley and serve.

Serves 6

Braised Brisket of Beef

1 beef brisket, 3–4 lb (1.5–2 kg)

½ teaspoon salt

1 teaspoon freshly ground pepper

2 teaspoons sweet paprika

4 tablespoons (2 oz/60 g) unsalted butter

4 large onions, diced

2 cups (16 fl oz/500 ml) canned tomato purée

8 large carrots, peeled and cut into 3-inch (7.5-cm) lengths (optional)

1 lb (500 g) fresh mushrooms, cut into quarters if large (optional)

Brisket is one of the best cuts for pot roast because the meat is marbled with fat and remains tender and moist during long, slow cooking. Don't worry about the absence of liquid in this recipe; the meat and onions give off considerable juice. Serve with potato pancakes or mashed potatoes and hot mustard. The optional carrots and mushrooms make fine accompaniments.

◆◊

Rub the brisket on both sides with the salt, pepper and paprika.

Melt 2 tablespoons of the butter in a large, heavy frying pan over high heat. Add the brisket and brown on both sides, about 15 minutes. Set aside.

Melt the remaining 2 tablespoons butter in a large, heavy pot over medium heat. Add the onions and cook, stirring, until soft and golden, 15–20 minutes. Place the brisket atop the onions and cover the pot. Reduce the heat to low and simmer for 1½ hours. The meat will give off quite a bit of liquid.

Add the tomato purée, cover and continue to simmer until the meat is tender, about 1 hour longer. If desired, add the carrot chunks and mushrooms during the last 30 minutes of cooking.

Transfer the meat to a platter and let stand for about 10 minutes. If you have added the carrots and mushrooms, transfer them with a slotted spoon to a serving bowl or the platter. Taste and adjust the seasoning of the pan juices and pour into a bowl. Slice the brisket across the grain and serve with the vegetables and pan juices.

Serves 6

Sicilian Stuffed Steak Rolls

FOR THE FILLING:

1 lb (500 g) ground (minced) beef or veal

3 slices bread, soaked in water, squeezed dry and crumbled

3 eggs

4 tablespoons chopped fresh parsley

2 tablespoons chopped fresh oregano or marjoram

¼ cup (1 oz/30 g) freshly grated Parmesan cheese

salt and freshly ground pepper

2 round steaks, each about 1½ lb (750 g) and cut about 1 inch (2.5 cm) thick

8 slices mortadella

4–6 hard-cooked eggs

¼ lb (125 g) salami, sliced and cut into strips 1 inch (2.5 cm) by ¼ inch (6 mm)

¼ lb (125 g) provolone cheese, cut into strips ½ inch (12 mm) wide, ½ inch (12 mm) thick and 2 inches (5 cm) long

5 tablespoons (3 fl oz/80 ml) olive oil

2 cups (8 oz/250 g) diced onion

4 cloves garlic, finely minced

1½ cups (12 fl oz/375 ml) dry red wine

4 cups (32 fl oz/1 l) puréed canned tomatoes

2 tablespoons tomato paste

The name of this dish is farsu magru, *or "false lean"; it is a poor man's way of enriching and stretching a simple cut of meat. In Sicily this is served on special occasions and may be prepared with beef or veal. This recipe produces a great sauce that is ideal for a pasta accompaniment such as rigatoni or penne. Serve the steak rolls with broccoli or Swiss chard for a colorful and festive dinner.*

Combine all of the ingredients for the filling in a bowl, including salt and pepper to taste. Mix well and set aside.

Place the round steaks between sheets of plastic wrap and pound gently with a meat pounder until they are ½ inch (12 mm) thick. Layer half of the filling atop each of the steaks and press down in an even layer. Place the mortadella in a single layer atop the filling. Place 2 or 3 hard-cooked eggs in a row down the center of each steak and surround them with the strips of salami and cheese. Carefully roll up each steak like a log and tie in several places with kitchen string.

Warm 3 tablespoons of the oil in a frying pan over high heat. Brown the rolls on all sides, 15–20 minutes. Set aside.

In a heavy pot that is large enough to hold the 2 beef rolls, warm the remaining 2 tablespoons oil over medium heat. Add the onion and cook until tender and translucent, 10–15 minutes. Add the garlic, wine, tomatoes and tomato paste and bring to a simmer. Add the beef rolls, reduce the heat to low, cover and simmer until the beef is tender, about 1½ hours.

Transfer the beef rolls to a platter and let stand for a few minutes. Season the sauce to taste with salt and pepper. Snip the strings from the beef rolls and slice crosswise ½ inch (12 mm) thick. Serve the sauce in a bowl alongside.

Makes 2 steak rolls; serves 6–8

Texas Beef Chili

FOR THE BEANS:

1 cup (7 oz/220 g) dried pinto or kidney
   beans
1 onion, chopped
2 cloves garlic, minced
1 teaspoon dried oregano
salt

FOR THE CHILI:

4 tablespoons (2 fl oz/60 ml) olive oil, lard
   or bacon drippings
2 lb (1 kg) beef chuck, cut into ½-inch
   (12-mm) cubes
2 onions, chopped
4 cloves garlic, minced
1 tablespoon dried oregano
1 teaspoon ground cumin
3 tablespoons chili powder
1 teapoon salt
1 teaspoon freshly ground black
   pepper
½ teaspoon cayenne pepper, or to taste
1 can (6 oz/185 g) tomato paste
2 cups (12 oz/375 g) diced, canned plum
   (Roma) tomatoes with their juices
1½ cups (12 fl oz/375 ml) beer, water or
   beef stock (*preferably homemade, see
   page 9*)

Although many chili recipes use ground (minced) beef, dicing the meat produces a more interesting dish. Some chili lovers add the beans to the meat, but purists serve the beans on the side. The garnishes for this chili are half the fun. Serve with warm corn tortillas, sour cream, sliced avocado and salsa. Finely minced onion and cilantro (fresh coriander) may be sprinkled on top, if desired.

❖

*T*o prepare the beans, place them in a bowl, add water to cover and refrigerate overnight. Drain and place in a saucepan. Add water to cover by about 1 inch (2.5 cm). Add the onion, garlic and oregano, cover partially and simmer until tender, about 1 hour. Add salt to taste and set aside.

To prepare the chili, warm 2 tablespoons of the oil or fat in a heavy saucepan over high heat. Working in batches, add the meat and brown on all sides, 8–10 minutes. Set aside.

Warm the remaining 2 tablespoons oil in a large, heavy pot over medium heat. Add the onions and cook until soft and pale gold, 15–20 minutes. Add the garlic, oregano, cumin, chili powder, salt, black pepper and cayenne pepper; simmer for 1–2 minutes. Stir in the tomato paste and tomatoes and their liquid. Add the reserved beef and the beer or other liquid; bring to a boil, reduce the heat, cover and simmer until the beef is tender, about 1 hour.

Serve the beans on the side or stir into the chili and simmer together for about 15 minutes.

Serves 6

Veal Ragout with Mushrooms and Cream

about 1 cup (4 oz/125 g) all-purpose (plain) flour

salt, freshly ground pepper and freshly grated nutmeg

3 lb (1.5 kg) veal shoulder or meat cut from the shank (shin), cut into 2-inch (5-cm) cubes

½ cup (4 fl oz/125 ml) plus 1 tablespoon olive oil, or half unsalted butter and half olive oil

1 large onion, diced

1 teaspoon finely minced garlic

2 teaspoons chopped fresh thyme

6 cups (48 fl oz/1.5 l) chicken stock

18–24 pearl onions, unpeeled

1 lb (500 g) small white or brown fresh cultivated mushrooms or chanterelles or other wild mushrooms, or a combination, stemmed

2 egg yolks, optional

½–1 cup (4–8 fl oz/125–250 ml) heavy (double) cream

3–4 tablespoons (about 2 fl oz/60 ml) fresh lemon juice, or to taste

minced fresh parsley for garnish

If you like, add ¼ cup (½ oz/15 g) dried, sliced porcini mushrooms, soaked to soften and drained, with the fresh mushrooms. Serve with spinach noodles. The optional egg yolks produce a richer dish.

❖

Mix the flour and salt, pepper and nutmeg to taste on a plate and use to coat the veal. Warm ¼ cup (2 fl oz/60 ml) of the oil (or half oil and half butter) in a large frying pan. Working in batches, add the veal and brown on all sides, about 10 minutes, adding more oil as needed. Set aside.

Warm 2 tablespoons of the remaining oil (or half oil and half butter) in a large, heavy pot over low heat. Add the onion and sauté until tender, 10–15 minutes. Add the garlic and 1 teaspoon thyme and sauté a few minutes. Add the veal and 5 cups (40 fl oz/1.25 l) stock. Bring to a boil, reduce the heat to low, cover and simmer until the veal is tender, 1–1¼ hours.

Meanwhile, peel the pearl onions as directed in the glossary (see page 106). In a saucepan bring the remaining stock to a boil, add the onions, cover and boil until tender, 10–15 minutes. At the same time, in a large frying pan over high heat, warm the remaining 3 tablespoons oil (or half oil and half butter). Add the mushrooms and brown quickly, 2–3 minutes.

Add the onions and mushrooms and their liquid and the remaining 1 teaspoon thyme to the veal during the last 10 minutes of cooking. Just before serving, stir together the yolks, if using, cream and lemon juice, then stir into the veal. Simmer, stirring, to thicken a bit. Do not boil if yolks have been added; reduce pan juices if only cream has been added. Adjust the seasoning, sprinkle with parsley and serve.

Serves 6

Stuffed Cabbage

2 green cabbages, about 2 lb (1 kg) total weight

FOR THE FILLING:
1 onion, coarsely chopped
2 eggs
1½ lb (750 g) ground (minced) beef chuck
2 cups (14 oz/440 g) long-grain white rice
salt and freshly ground pepper

1 onion, diced
1 cup (8 fl oz/250 ml) beef stock (*preferably homemade, see page 9*) or water
3 cups (24 fl oz/750 ml) canned tomato purée
½ cup (4 fl oz/125 ml) fresh lemon juice, or more to taste
1 cup (7 oz/220 g) firmly packed brown sugar, or more to taste
salt and freshly ground pepper

This is one of those homey peasant dishes that everyone loves and rarely can find on a restaurant menu. It is worth the effort and is best made the day before and reheated. Serve with good dark bread to sop up the juices.

❖

Using a sharp knife remove the central tough core of the cabbage. Bring a large pot filled with salted water to a boil and drop in the cabbages, one at a time. Simmer until the leaves loosen and are pliable, about 10 minutes. Transfer to a colander. When they are cool enough to handle, pull off the largest leaves, being careful not to tear them, and set aside. You'll need about 24 leaves. (Use the centers of the cabbages in a vegetable dish or add to a soup.)

To prepare the filling, in a blender or in a food processor fitted with the metal blade, combine the onion and eggs and purée until smooth. Place the beef and rice in a bowl, add the egg mixture and mix well. Season to taste with salt and pepper. Place 1 or 2 heaping tablespoons of filling on each cabbage leaf. Fold in the sides, roll up and skewer closed with a toothpick.

In a deep, wide pot combine the onion, stock or water, tomato purée, lemon juice and sugar. Bring to a simmer over medium heat, stirring to dissolve the sugar. Slip in the cabbage rolls, wait until the liquid returns to a gentle simmer, cover and simmer over low heat on the stove top or in an oven preheated to 325°F (165°C) until the filling is fully cooked, about 2½ hours. Baste occasionally with the cooking liquid.

Using a slotted spoon, transfer the rolls to a warmed platter or individual bowls. Adjust the sweet-and-sour flavor of the pan juices, if necessary, with more sugar and lemon juice. Season to taste with salt and pepper. Spoon the pan juices over the rolls and serve.

Serves 6–8

Boiled Beef

1 beef brisket, 3–4 lb (1.5–2 kg)

3 carrots, peeled and sliced

3 celery stalks, sliced, about 1 cup (4 oz/125 g)

2 cloves garlic, sliced

4 onions, cut in half

about 12 peppercorns

1 fresh thyme sprig

1 bay leaf

about 8 cups (64 fl oz/2 l) beef stock (*preferably homemade, see page 9*) or water

While this recipe is simplicity itself, there is good reason to enrich it a bit by braising the beef in stock rather than water. The meat and vegetables will be more flavorful and the resulting broth will be a rich treat for sipping or for cooking. Whole leeks, potatoes or carrots are especially good poached in this liquid. Serve the beef with hot mustard, caper sauce (recipe on page 14) or cold horseradish cream (page 13).

❖

Combine all of the ingredients in a large, heavy saucepan, adding enough stock or water to cover. Bring to a boil, reduce the heat to low, cover and simmer until the meat is tender, 3–4 hours. Occasionally skim off any scum and froth from the surface.

Transfer the meat to a platter and let stand for about 10 minutes. Strain the cooking juices and reserve for cooking other dishes or for reheating any leftover boiled beef. Slice the beef across the grain for serving.

Serves 6

Picadillo

4 tablespoons (2 fl oz/60 ml) olive oil

1 lb (500 g) ground (minced) beef chuck

2 onions, chopped

4 celery stalks, chopped

4 cloves garlic, finely minced

½ cup (2½ oz/75 g) diced, seeded fresh
   pasilla or poblano chili peppers
   (¼-inch/6-mm dice)

2 teaspoons ground cumin

¼ teaspoon ground cloves

1 teaspoon ground cinnamon

½ cup (4 fl oz/125 ml) dry red wine, or
   as needed

1 cup (6 oz/185 g) diced, canned plum
   (Roma) tomatoes

⅔ cup (4 oz/125 g) raisins, soaked in hot
   water to cover for 20 minutes and
   drained

¼ cup (2 oz/60 g) pimiento-stuffed
   olives, cut in half crosswise

beef stock (*preferably homemade, see page 9*)
   as needed, optional

salt and freshly ground pepper

1 hard-cooked egg, coarsely chopped,
   optional

½ cup (2 oz/60 g) lightly toasted chopped
   almonds, optional

A traditional Cuban beef hash that can be served with rice, black beans, greens and fried plantains. This spicy meat mixture also makes a great filling for roast chicken or peppers (capsicums). To prepare the stuffed peppers, cut off a thin slice from the stem end of each pepper and scoop out the seeds. Stuff the cooked meat mixture into the peppers and stand them upright in a baking dish just large enough to accommodate them. Add a little water to the dish, cover tightly with aluminum foil and bake in a preheated 350°F (180°C) oven until the peppers are tender when pierced with a fork, about 30 minutes.

◈

Warm 2 tablespoons of the oil in a large frying pan over high heat. Add the beef and cook, breaking it up with a wooden spoon, until browned, 10–15 minutes. Transfer the meat and pan juices to a bowl and set aside.

Warm the remaining 2 tablespoons oil in the same pan over medium heat. Add the onions, celery, garlic and chili peppers and cook, stirring occasionally, until the vegetables soften, about 10 minutes. Add the beef and its juices, cumin, cloves, cinnamon, wine, tomatoes, raisins and olives. Reduce the heat to low and simmer, uncovered, for about 15 minutes. If too dry, add a little more wine or some beef stock, a bit at a time. Season to taste with salt and pepper.

Sprinkle with chopped hard-cooked egg or toasted almonds, if you like, and serve.

Serves 4

Deviled Short Ribs

½ cup (4 oz/125 g) Dijon mustard, or
   more to taste
1 tablespoon salt
2 tablespoons chili powder
4 teaspoons brown sugar
¼ cup (2 fl oz/60 ml) fresh lemon juice
1 tablespoon grated lemon zest
4 cloves garlic, minced
2 cups (8 oz/250 g) diced onion
1 teaspoon ground allspice or ½ teaspoon
   ground cloves
2 teaspoons freshly ground black pepper
½ cup (4 fl oz/125 ml) olive oil
6 lb (3 kg) short ribs, cut into serving
   pieces
1 cup (8 fl oz/250 ml) beef stock
   (*preferably homemade, see page 9*)

Oven-barbecued short ribs are best served with simple baked potatoes and greens. Marinate the ribs for at least 6 hours, or preferably overnight.

◆◇

*I*n a large bowl combine all of the ingredients except the ribs and stock. Mix well, add the ribs, cover and refrigerate for at least 6 hours, or as long as overnight, turning the ribs occasionally.

   Preheat an oven to 450°F (230°C). Drain the ribs and reserve the marinade. Place the ribs on a rack in a roasting pan and bake until browned, about 30 minutes. Reduce the heat to 350°F (180°C). Pour the reserved marinade evenly over the ribs and bake until tender, about 1½ hours longer.

   Transfer the ribs to a warmed platter and keep warm. Drain off the excess fat from the roasting pan and place the pan on the stove top over high heat. Pour in the stock and deglaze the pan by stirring to dislodge any browned bits. Boil for 2 minutes; adjust the seasoning with salt and pepper and add more mustard, if you like. Pour the sauce over the short ribs and serve at once.

Serves 6

Sumatran Beef Ragout

peanut oil as needed

3 lb (1.5 kg) stewing beef such as chuck, cut into 1½-inch (4-cm) cubes

4–5 cups (1–1¼ lb/500–625 g) diced onions (about 3 large)

3 tablespoons grated fresh ginger

2 tablespoons finely minced garlic

1 teaspoon finely minced fresh jalapeño pepper, or to taste

1 teaspoon ground turmeric

2 tablespoons ground coriander

2 bay leaves

2 long strips lemon zest or 2 stalks fresh lemongrass, crushed and cut into 3-inch (7.5-cm) lengths

3 cups (24 fl oz/750 ml) coconut milk

2 cups (16 fl oz/500 ml) beef stock (preferably homemade, see page 9)

salt and freshly ground pepper

A rich and flavorful beef curry called kalio. *Serve with rice and green beans seasoned with ginger or toasted coconut.*

❖

Place a frying pan over high heat and pour in enough oil to form a film on the bottom. Working in batches, add the beef and fry over high heat until browned on all sides, 10–15 minutes. Set aside.

Warm 3 tablespoons oil in a large, heavy pot over medium heat. Add the onions and cook until tender and translucent, 10–15 minutes. Add the ginger, garlic, jalapeño, turmeric, coriander, bay leaves and lemon zest or lemongrass and cook for 5 minutes longer.

Add the beef to the pot, along with the coconut milk and stock. Bring to a simmer, cover and cook until the meat is very tender, about 3 hours.

Discard the lemongrass; season to taste with salt and pepper.

Serves 6

Sauerbraten

2 teaspoons dry mustard

1 teaspoon salt

½ teaspoon freshly ground pepper

½ teaspoon ground cloves

3 tablespoons brown sugar

3 tablespoons red wine vinegar

2 cups (16 fl oz/500 ml) dry red wine

¼ cup (2 fl oz/60 ml) canned tomato
   purée

1 teaspoon Worcestershire sauce

8 gingersnaps, crushed, plus more if
   needed for pan juices

2 onions, thinly sliced

3 cloves garlic, minced

2 cups (16 fl oz/500 ml) beef stock
   (preferably homemade, see page 9)

1 top round (rump) roast, 3–4 lb
   (1.5–2 kg)

1 cup (5 oz/155 g) raisins, optional

*Rich and savory, this German sweet-and-sour pot roast is best
served with braised red cabbage and potato pancakes. Applesauce
can be a condiment, or serve sliced sautéed apples. You will need
to plan ahead to make this dish, as the meat must marinate for
2–3 days.*

Combine the dry mustard, salt, pepper, cloves and brown
sugar in a large, deep bowl. Whisk in the vinegar and wine.
Add the tomato purée, Worcestershire sauce, gingersnaps,
onions, garlic and stock. Mix well and add the beef. Cover and
refrigerate for 2–3 days, turning the beef occasionally.

   Place the beef and all of the marinade in a large, heavy pot.
Bring to a boil, reduce the heat to low, cover and simmer until
the meat is tender, about 2½ hours. Add the raisins, if using,
during the last 30 minutes.

   Transfer the beef to a platter and let stand for about 10
minutes. If the pan juices are thin, crumble in a few more
gingersnaps and reduce over high heat. Taste and adjust the
seasoning. Pour into a bowl and serve alongside the beef.
Slice the beef across the grain.

Serves 6

Ossobuco alla Milanese

about 1½ cups (6 oz/180 g) all-purpose
 (plain) flour
salt and freshly ground pepper
6 meaty veal shanks (shins), each about
 1½ lb (750 g), each sawed crosswise
 into 2 pieces
½ cup (4 fl oz/125 ml) olive oil, or as
 needed
½ cup (4 oz/125 g) unsalted butter
4 cups (1 lb/500 g) diced onions (about
 3 large)
1½ cups (8 oz/250 g) diced, peeled
 carrots
1½ cups (8 oz/250 g) diced celery
1 cup (8 fl oz/250 ml) dry white wine
4 cups (2 lb/1 kg) diced plum (Roma)
 tomatoes
3–4 cups (24–32 fl oz/750 ml–1 l) beef
 stock (*preferably homemade, see page 9*)
salt and freshly ground pepper

FOR THE GREMOLATA:
2 teaspoons finely minced garlic
2 tablespoons grated or shredded lemon
 zest
5 tablespoons chopped fresh parsley
1 tablespoon grated or shredded orange
 zest, optional

Ossobuco means "bone with a hole." In the classic ossobuco alla milanese, veal shanks are braised with aromatic vegetables, wine, stock and occasionally with a little tomato. If you have special marrow spoons, set them at the table for guests to dig the succulent marrow from the center of the shanks. Saffron risotto is the classic accompaniment, or serve with buttered saffron fettuccine. If peas are in season, add them to the rice or noodles.

Place the flour on a plate and season to taste with salt and pepper. Coat the veal shanks with the flour.

 Warm ¼ cup (2 fl oz/60 ml) of the oil in a large, heavy frying pan over high heat. Add as many veal shanks as will fit comfortably and brown on all sides, 15–20 minutes. Transfer to a plate and add the remaining oil to the pan. Brown the remaining shanks in the same way. Set aside.

 In a large, heavy pot or deep sauté pan, melt the butter over medium heat. Add the onions, carrots and celery and cook, stirring, until tender, about 15 minutes. Place the veal shanks on top of the vegetables and pour in the wine, tomatoes and the stock to cover. Bring to a boil, reduce the heat to low, cover and simmer on the stove top or in an oven preheated to 350°F (180°C) until the veal is very tender, 1–1¼ hours. The meat should be almost falling off the bones.

 Season the vegetable sauce to taste with salt and pepper. Combine the gremolata ingredients in a small bowl, mix well and sprinkle over the shanks. Cook for 5 minutes longer and serve with the sauce.

Serves 6

Corned Beef

1 corned beef brisket, 4–5 lb (2–2.5 kg)
cold water as needed
3 qt (3 l) water, boiling
2 onions, each stuck with 3 whole cloves
2 carrots, peeled
2 bay leaves
3 fresh parsley sprigs
12 peppercorns, crushed
12 coriander seeds
1 cinnamon stick, about 1 inch (2.5 cm)
   long

This recipe discards the first batch of cooking water after an hour and starts the corned beef again with fresh hot water to mimimize saltiness. Serve with hot mustard and boiled new potatoes. Traditionalists may add a head of green cabbage cut into 6 wedges to the pot during the last 15 minutes of cooking, but torn cabbage leaves, stir-fried with lemon zest and toasted pine nuts, are a lighter and more interesting vegetable accompaniment. Any leftover beef makes great sandwiches.

❖

*P*lace the corned beef in a large, heavy pot and add cold water to cover. Bring to a boil, reduce the heat, cover and simmer for 1 hour. Pour off the water.

Add the boiling water, onions and carrots. Bring back to a boil and skim off any scum or froth from the surface. Add all the remaining ingredients, reduce the heat, cover and simmer until the meat is tender but firm, 2–4 hours. After 2 hours, occasionally test the beef with a skewer for doneness. When it pierces easily, it is ready.

Drain the meat. Place on a platter and let stand for about 10 minutes. Slice across the grain and serve.

Serves 6

Beef Paprikash

½ cup (4 oz/120 g) unsalted butter, lard or bacon drippings

3 lb (1.5 kg) beef chuck, cut into 2-inch (5-cm) cubes

salt and freshly ground pepper

5 tablespoons sweet Hungarian paprika

2 large onions, chopped

3 cloves garlic, minced

2 tablespoons tomato paste

2 cups (16 fl oz/500 ml) beef stock (*preferably homemade, see page 9*)

1–1½ cups (8–12 fl oz/250–375 ml) sour cream, at room temperature

½ cup (¾ oz/20 g) chopped fresh dill

Sautéed peppers and fresh dill make a colorful, tasty garnish for this hearty Hungarian ragout. Lard is traditionally used for browning the meat, but you may use butter or even bacon drippings if you prefer. Bring the sour cream to room temperature so that it won't curdle when it is added to the stew. Serve with buttered noodles or simple boiled potatoes.

Warm ¼ cup (2 oz/60 g) of the butter or fat in a heavy frying pan over high heat. Sprinkle the beef with salt and pepper to taste and 1 tablespoon of the paprika. Brown the meat on all sides, about 15 minutes. Set aside.

In a large, heavy pot, warm the remaining ¼ cup (2 oz/60 g) butter or fat over medium heat. Add the onions and sauté until tender and translucent, 10–15 minutes. Add the garlic and the remaining 4 tablespoons (2 oz/60 g) paprika and cook for a few minutes longer. Add the tomato paste, stock and reserved beef. Bring to a boil, reduce to low, cover and simmer until the beef is tender, about 2½ hours.

Taste and adjust the seasoning. Remove from the heat and stir in the sour cream and dill. Serve hot.

Serves 6

Beef Tongue with Sweet-Sour Sauce

1 beef tongue, about 3 lb (1.5 kg), well scrubbed

boiling water as needed

2 onions

1 large carrot, peeled

3 celery stalks with leaves

12 peppercorns

1 bay leaf

6 coriander seeds

5 tablespoons (2½ oz/80 g) unsalted butter

3 tablespoons all-purpose (plain) flour

¼ teaspoon ground ginger

2½ cups (20 fl oz/625 ml) beef stock, heated (*preferably homemade, see page 9*) or 1¾ cups (14 fl oz/440 ml) beef stock and ¾ cup (6 fl oz/185 ml) tongue cooking liquid

2 tablespoons red wine vinegar

½ cup (4 fl oz/125 ml) Marsala

grated or shredded zest of 1 lemon

grated or shredded zest of 1 orange

½ cup (2 oz/60 g) toasted sliced almonds

½ cup (3 oz/90 g) raisins, soaked in hot water or Marsala to cover for 20 minutes

salt and freshly ground pepper

For tongue aficionados. The sweet-and-sour sauce with toasted almonds makes a fine contrast to the meat. Rice pilaf mixed with green (spring) onions is a good accompaniment. Or you may cook the tongue without making the sweet-sour sauce and serve it with caper sauce (recipe on page 14) or cold horseradish cream (page 13) and boiled potatoes. Leftover tongue makes great sandwiches, paired with Gruyère cheese and hot mustard.

❖

Place the tongue in a deep, heavy pot and add boiling water to cover. Add the onions, carrot, celery, peppercorns, bay leaf and coriander seeds. Cover and simmer over low heat until tender, about 3 hours. Transfer the tongue to a plate. Peel the skin from the tongue and trim off the fat, gristle and any small bones. Keep warm. If you plan to use the cooking liquid to make the sauce, strain it and keep it hot.

Melt the butter in a saucepan over medium heat. Add the flour and ginger and cook, stirring, until smooth but not browned, about 3 minutes. Add the stock or stock–cooking liquid mixture, stirring or whisking occasionally until it comes to a boil. Reduce the heat and whisk in the vinegar and Marsala. Stir in the zests, almonds and raisins with their soaking liquid; simmer for about 10 minutes. Season to taste with salt and pepper.

Slice the tongue and serve on a warmed platter. Spoon the sauce over the top.

Serves 6–8

Greek Beef Stew

½ cup (4 fl oz/120 ml) olive oil

3 lb (1.5 kg) beef chuck, cut into 2-inch (5-cm) cubes

salt and freshly ground pepper

2 large onions, chopped

6 cloves garlic, minced

2 teaspoons ground cinnamon

1 teaspoon ground cloves

3 cups (24 fl oz/750 ml) dry red wine

10 fresh or canned plum (Roma) tomatoes, peeled, seeded and chopped, or 3 cups (24 fl oz/750 ml) canned tomato purée

2 bay leaves

2 lb (1 kg) pearl onions, unpeeled

¾ cup (4 oz/125 g) dried currants

Sweet and aromatic with currants, cinnamon, cloves and tomatoes, this Greek beef stew, called stifatho, *is best served with pilaf or oven-roasted potatoes. Some crumbled feta cheese is a flavorful garnish. The stew can simmer on the stove top or in the oven. If you have time, marinate the beef, which will give it more flavor: Combine 1 teaspoon of the cinnamon, ½ teaspoon of the cloves and 1 cup (8 fl oz/250 ml) of the red wine in a large, deep bowl. Add the beef, cover and refrigerate overnight, turning the beef occasionally. Drain, reserving the marinade, and dry the meat well before browning.*

❖

Warm ¼ cup (2 fl oz/60 ml) of the oil in a frying pan over high heat. Sprinkle the meat with salt and pepper to taste and brown on all sides, 10–15 minutes. Set aside.

In a large, heavy pot warm the remaining ¼ cup (2 fl oz/ 60 ml) oil over medium heat. Add the chopped onions and sauté until tender and translucent, 10–15 minutes. Add the garlic, cinnamon and cloves and cook for a few more minutes. Add the browned beef cubes, wine, tomatoes or tomato purée and bay leaves (and the reserved marinade, if you have it) and bring to a boil. Reduce the heat to low, cover and simmer until the meat is tender, 1½–2 hours. Alternatively, place in an oven preheated to 325°F (165°C) for the same amount of time.

Once the meat is cooking, peel the pearl onions as directed in the glossary (see page 106). Add the onions and currants to the stew during the last 45 minutes of cooking. Taste and adjust the seasoning just before serving.

Serves 6

Braised Rolled Leg of Veal

2 eggs

3 tablespoons chopped fresh parsley

1 teaspoon chopped fresh thyme

salt and freshly ground pepper

6 tablespoons (3 fl oz/90 ml) olive oil

2 small bunches spinach, trimmed and carefully washed (about 4 cups/4 oz/ 125 g leaves)

1 teaspoon freshly grated nutmeg

1 leg of veal, boned and butterflied, about 4 lb (2 kg)

6 slices pancetta or prosciutto

2 cloves garlic, cut into slivers

3 cups (12 oz/375 g) diced onions

¾ cup (4 oz/125 g) diced, peeled carrot

½ cup (2½ oz/75 g) diced celery

1½ cups (12 fl oz/375 ml) dry white wine

2 cups (16 fl oz/500 ml) chicken, veal or beef stock (*preferably homemade, see page 9*)

This dish is a little bit of work, but worth the effort. Ask your butcher to bone and butterfly the leg for you. Serve with noodles or mashed potatoes.

❖

*I*n a small bowl whisk together the eggs, parsley, thyme and salt and pepper to taste. Warm 2 tablespoons of the oil in a wide sauté pan over high heat. Pour in the eggs in a thin sheet; stir occasionally until set. Slip onto a plate; set aside.

Place the spinach in a sauté pan with only the water clinging to the leaves. Cover and cook over medium heat, stirring, until wilted, about 3 minutes. Drain and press out moisture; chop finely and season with salt, pepper and ½ teaspoon of the nutmeg; set aside.

Trim the gristle, tendons and excess fat from the veal leg. Place between sheets of plastic wrap and pound gently to an even thickness. Sprinkle with salt, pepper and the remaining ½ teaspoon nutmeg. Cover the leg completely with the pancetta or prosciutto. Top with the omelet and spinach. Roll up and tie with kitchen string. Poke in several places with a knife and insert the garlic slivers into the slits. Sprinkle with salt and pepper. Warm 2 tablespoons of the oil in a frying pan over high heat. Add the veal and brown on all sides, about 10 minutes.

Warm the remaining 2 tablespoons oil in a large, heavy pot over medium heat. Add the onions, carrot and celery and sauté until soft, 10–15 minutes. Add the veal, wine and stock and bring to a boil. Reduce the heat to low, cover and simmer on the stove top or in an oven preheated to 325°F (165°C) until the veal is tender or a meat thermometer registers 140°F (60°C), about 1½ hours.

Transfer to a warmed platter; let stand for 10 minutes. Discard the string and cut into slices ⅓ inch (8 mm) thick. Season the vegetables and pan juices and serve in a bowl on the side.

Serves 6

Onion-Stuffed Beef Kefta

FOR THE FILLING:

2 tablespoons unsalted butter or olive oil
   or peanut oil
1 large onion, finely chopped (about
   1½ cups/8 oz/250 g)
2 teaspoons grated fresh ginger
1 teaspoon finely minced fresh jalapeño
   pepper, or to taste
4 tablespoons finely chopped fresh mint
grated zest of 1 lemon
salt and freshly ground pepper

FOR THE MEAT MIXTURE:

1 lb (500 g) ground (minced) beef chuck
1 tablespoon finely minced garlic
1 teaspoon ground cinnamon
2 teaspoons ground cumin
1 teaspoon salt
½ teaspoon freshly ground pepper
¼ teaspoon cayenne pepper
½ teaspoon ground ginger

olive oil or peanut oil for frying
salt

While Indian-style ground meat kebabs are traditionally made with lamb, they are excellent when made with ground beef. The spicy onion stuffing adds a texture and taste contrast. The beef patties may also be broiled. Serve with pita bread and a raita of plain yogurt, diced tomatoes and cucumbers flavored with toasted cumin seeds.

❧

To prepare the filling, warm the butter or oil in a sauté pan over medium heat. Add the onion and sauté until half-cooked and almost translucent, 3–5 minutes. Add the ginger and jalapeño and sauté for 1 or 2 minutes longer. Remove from the heat and mix in the mint and lemon zest. Season to taste with salt and pepper. Transfer to a bowl, cover and chill.

In a bowl combine all the ingredients for the meat mixture and mix well with your hands. Cover and chill.

When the meat mixture and the filling are well chilled, divide the meat mixture in half. Form one half into 4 patties, each about ½ inch (12 mm) thick. Make a well in the center of each patty and stuff one-fourth of the onion filling into the well. Top each patty with one-fourth of the remaining meat. Shape each portion into an oval about 3 inches (7.5 cm) long.

Lightly oil a large, heavy frying pan and heat until very hot. Sprinkle lightly with salt. When the salt starts to brown, add the meat ovals. Fry, turning once, until crusty and browned, about 3 minutes on each side. Do not overcook; they should be quite juicy.

Serves 4

Veal alla Parmigiana

1½ lb (750 g) veal scallops, about ½ inch (12 mm) thick
about ¾ cup (3 oz/90 g) all-purpose (plain) flour
salt and freshly ground pepper
½ cup (2 oz/60 g) freshly grated Parmesan cheese
¼ cup (2 fl oz/60 ml) olive oil
8–12 thin slices fresh mozzarella
1 cup (8 fl oz/250 ml) basic tomato sauce, heated (*recipe on page 14*)

Despite its name, this classic veal dish is from the Italian south. Parmesan cheese does come from the north, but this mixture of mozzarella and tomato speaks of Naples. Serve this with sautéed or broiled eggplant (aubergine) or zucchini (courgettes). Or sauté eggplant slices and lay them atop the sautéed veal, then cover with the mozzarella.

*P*lace the veal scallops between 2 sheets of plastic wrap and pound gently with a meat pounder until about ¼ inch (6 mm) thick. Place the flour on a plate and season with salt and pepper and a few tablespoons of the Parmesan. Dip the veal in the seasoned flour and shake off any excess.

Heat the oil in a large sauté pan over medium-high heat. Add the veal, in batches if necessary, and brown lightly on one side, about 2 minutes. Turn the veal, brown on the second side for 1 minute and top with the mozzarella slices. Reduce the heat to low, cover and cook until the cheese softens, about 2 minutes.

Transfer the veal to individual plates and spoon a little tomato sauce over the top. Sprinkle with the remaining Parmesan and serve.

Serves 4

Moroccan Meatballs

FOR THE MEATBALLS:

1 lb (500 g) ground (minced) beef chuck

2 teaspoons ground cumin

1 tablespoon paprika

½ teaspoon cayenne pepper

½ teaspoon freshly ground pepper

½ teaspoon ground cinnamon

¼ teaspoon ground ginger

4 tablespoons finely minced fresh parsley

3 tablespoons finely minced fresh cilantro (fresh coriander)

1 teaspoon salt

1 small onion, grated or finely chopped

2 tablespoons olive oil or peanut oil

FOR THE TOMATO SAUCE:

2 cups (1 lb/500 g) canned plum (Roma) tomatoes

2 tablespoons olive oil

2 onions, chopped

4 cloves garlic, minced

2 teaspoons ground cumin

pinch of cayenne pepper

½ teaspoon freshly ground black pepper

½ cup (¾ oz/20 g) chopped fresh parsley, mint or cilantro (fresh coriander), or a mixture

1 cup (8 fl oz/250 ml) canned tomato purée

The beef for this recipe should not be too lean or the meatballs will be dry. Top the meatballs with poached eggs, if you like, and serve with couscous. You may also omit the tomato sauce, form the meat mixture into oval patties and sauté or grill the patties; serve them with pita bread and harissa, *the fiery North African chili sauce. For "instant* harissa," *whisk together 2 tablespoons ground cumin, 2 teaspoons cayenne pepper, 3 tablespoons fresh lemon juice, ½ cup (4 fl oz/125 ml) olive oil, 1 teaspoon ground caraway (if desired) and salt to taste.*

*I*n a bowl combine all of the ingredients for the meatballs. Using your hands, mix well. Form into balls 1 inch (2.5 cm) in diameter.

In a large frying pan over high heat, warm the oil. Add the meatballs and brown on all sides, 8–10 minutes. Remove from the heat and set aside.

To prepare the sauce, place the tomatoes with some of their juice in a food processor fitted with the metal blade and process until finely chopped. Set aside. Heat the oil in a large sauté pan over medium heat. Add the onions and sauté until tender and translucent, 10–15 minutes. Add the garlic, cumin, cayenne, black pepper and parsley and/or other herb(s) and sauté for 5 minutes longer. Add the browned meatballs, the reserved tomatoes and the tomato purée and cook for 15 minutes longer. Serve hot.

Serves 4

Beef Hash

4 tablespoons (2 oz/60 g) unsalted butter

4 tablespoons (2 fl oz/60 ml) olive oil

2 cups (8 oz/250 g) diced onion

2½ cups (12 oz/375 g) diced, unpeeled boiling potatoes

4 cups (1¼ lb/625 g) diced leftover roast or corned beef (½-inch/12-mm dice)

salt and freshly ground pepper

2 teaspoons Worcestershire sauce, optional

Although many hash recipes use ground (minced) meat, the texture of hash is much better when the meat is diced by hand. You can use cooked corned beef for this recipe, in which case you'll need to add little or no salt. Dice the onions and potatoes a little smaller than the beef. The potatoes may be cooked, but the texture is better if you start with raw potatoes because they will get crispier. Serve with poached or fried eggs and chili sauce.

Warm 1 tablespoon of the butter and 2 tablespoons of the oil in a sauté pan over medium heat. Add the onion and sauté until golden, 15–20 minutes. Set aside.

In a large sauté pan, heat the remaining 3 tablespoons butter and 2 tablespoons oil and add the potatoes. Cook over medium-high heat, stirring often, until the potatoes are browned and crusty, about 15 minutes.

Add the reserved onion and the beef and cook until the mixture is crusty and browned, about 10 minutes longer. Season to taste with salt and pepper and mix in the Worcestershire sauce, if using. Serve at once.

Serves 4

Calves' Liver with Onions, Lemon and Sage

½ cup (4 fl oz/120 ml) olive oil

4 cups (14 oz/440 g) sliced red (Spanish) onions (about 3 large)

about ¾ cup (3 oz/90 g) all-purpose (plain) flour

salt and freshly ground pepper

1½ lb (750 g) calves' liver, trimmed of all gristle and cut into 8 slices, each about ⅓ inch (8 mm) thick

1 cup (8 fl oz/250 ml) chicken stock

8 fresh sage leaves

¼ cup (2 fl oz/60 ml) fresh lemon juice

This is a Venetian dish of sautéed liver and onions, lightened with lemon juice and perfumed with fresh sage. In Venice the liver is cut into tiny strips, but large slices are easier to cook and turn. Ask your butcher to slice it for you. Serve with polenta or potatoes.

*H*eat ¼ cup (2 fl oz/60 ml) of the oil in a large sauté pan over medium heat. Add the onions and sauté until tender and translucent, 10–15 minutes. Using a slotted spoon, transfer to a bowl and set aside.

Place the flour on a plate and season with salt and pepper. Dip the liver in the seasoned flour and shake off any excess. Heat the remaining ¼ cup (2 fl oz/60 ml) oil in the same sauté pan over high heat. Add the liver and sear, turning once, 2–3 minutes on each side for medium-rare, or until done to your liking. Transfer the liver to a plate and keep warm.

Pour off the excess oil from the pan. Pour in the stock over high heat and deglaze the pan by stirring to dislodge any browned bits. Boil until slightly thickened. Return the onions to the pan, add the sage leaves and lemon juice and cook for 2 minutes. Season to taste with salt and pepper.

To serve, place the liver on individual plates and spoon the onions over the top.

Serves 4

59

Deviled Hamburgers

1 lb (500 g) ground (minced) beef chuck
3 tablespoons grated onion
1 teaspoon Worcestershire sauce
2 teaspoons prepared hot mustard
2 cloves garlic, finely minced
½ teaspoon freshly ground pepper
¼ teaspoon cayenne pepper
olive oil or peanut oil for frying
salt

Just a glorified but glorious hamburger. If you like, add chili powder, bottled chili sauce or a little freshly grated horseradish to the meat mixture. Serve with sliced onions and toasted buns. Or serve on a plate with potato salad, coleslaw and pickles.

In a bowl combine all the ingredients except the oil and salt. Handling the meat gently, form into 4 round patties. The meat mixture should just hold together.

Lightly oil a large, heavy frying pan or stove-top griddle and heat until very hot. Sprinkle with salt. When the salt starts to brown, add the meat patties. Sear on one side and then flip with a spatula and brown the second side. Cook until done to your liking. Serve at once.

Serves 3–4

Red Wine–Marinated Fillets

2 cups (16 fl oz/500 ml) dry red wine
1 bay leaf
6 peppercorns, gently crushed
2 cloves garlic, smashed
2 whole cloves
1 allspice berry, gently crushed
2 fresh thyme sprigs
2 strips orange zest, each about 3 inches
    (7.5 cm) long
4 slices beef fillet, each about ½ lb (250 g)
    and cut about 1½ inches (4 cm) thick
1 cup (8 fl oz/250 ml) beef stock
    (*preferably homemade, see page 9*)
kosher salt
2–4 tablespoons unsalted butter

This dish tastes as if you'd worked for days. Actually it's just the red wine marinade that's working, and you get all the credit for a delicious and sophisticated steak. Pan-broiling is a simple technique for cooking meat or fish in a heavy frying pan with little or no oil or butter. A cast-iron pan works best. Serve with scalloped potatoes and grilled mushrooms.

Pour the wine into a small saucepan and bring to a simmer over medium heat. Add the bay leaf, peppercorns, garlic, cloves, allspice, thyme and orange zest and simmer for 15 minutes. Remove from the heat and let cool completely.

Place the fillets in a shallow dish and pour the wine mixture over the top. Cover and marinate at room temperature for up to 4 hours, or in the refrigerator as long as overnight.

Meanwhile, pour the beef stock into a small saucepan, bring to a boil and boil until reduced by half, about 20 minutes. Remove from the heat and set aside.

Remove the beef from the marinade, reserving the marinade. Pat dry with paper towels and sprinkle with a little kosher salt. Heat a heavy frying pan over high heat. Add the fillets and pan-broil until done to your liking, about 3 minutes on each side for rare. Remove from the pan and keep warm.

Pour 1 cup (8 fl oz/250 ml) of the marinade into the pan over high heat and deglaze by stirring to dislodge any browned bits. Boil until reduced by half. Add the reduced beef stock and reduce again by half. Swirl in the butter to smooth out the sauce and thicken it a bit. Spoon over the fillets and serve.

Serves 4

Veal Piccata

1 lb (500 g) veal scallops, about ½ inch (12 mm) thick

about ¾ cup (3 oz/90 g) all-purpose (plain) flour

salt and freshly ground pepper

2 tablespoons olive oil

4 tablespoons (2 oz/60 g) unsalted butter

1 cup (8 fl oz/250 ml) veal stock or beef stock (*preferably homemade, see page 9*)

3 tablespoons fresh lemon juice

¼ cup (2½ oz/75 g) capers, rinsed

2 tablespoons chopped fresh parsley

This is the simplest of veal scallop recipes. The veal should be cut from the leg and pounded gently. A simple deglazing of the pan with a little stock and lemon juice makes a tasty and light sauce. For a variation, add some fresh orange juice and grated orange zest to the pan when adding the capers and lemon juice. For a Milanese-style veal dish, dip the veal in beaten egg and then dried bread crumbs after flouring and sauté until golden; omit the lemon juice and capers and serve with lemon wedges. For veal with Marsala, deglaze the pan with half stock and half Marsala and omit the lemon juice and capers.

Place the veal scallops between 2 sheets of plastic wrap and pound gently with a meat pounder until they are about ¼ inch (6 mm) thick. Place the flour on a plate and season with salt and pepper. Dip the veal slices in the flour and shake off any excess.

Heat the oil and 2 tablespoons of the butter in a large sauté pan over high heat. Add the veal, in batches if necessary, and sauté, turning once, until golden on both sides, 2–3 minutes per side. Transfer to a warmed platter and keep warm.

Pour off the excess butter and oil from the pan. Pour in the stock and bring to a boil over high heat. Deglaze the pan by stirring to dislodge any browned bits. Boil until the stock is reduced by half. Swirl in the lemon juice and capers and then swirl in the remaining 2 tablespoons butter. Pour over the veal. Sprinkle with the parsley and serve at once.

Serves 4

Ginger Beef Stir-Fry

1 lb (500 g) flank steak, cut across the
grain into slices about 2½ inches (6 cm)
long and ⅛ inch (3 mm) thick
1 tablespoon soy sauce
1 tablespoon Asian sesame oil
1 tablespoon cornstarch (cornflour)
¼ lb (125 g) fresh ginger, peeled and cut
into matchstick strips (about ½ cup
strips)
1 teaspoon salt
1 cup (8 fl oz/250 ml) peanut oil
1 lb (500 g) asparagus, trimmed and cut
on the diagonal into slices ¼ inch
(6 mm) thick, optional
3 tablespoons water, if using asparagus
1 clove garlic, minced, optional
3 tablespoons sherry or rice wine
1 teaspoon sugar

*Fast, easy and economical. Although a large amount of oil is used to
cook the beef, the generous measure prevents sticking. The oil is then
poured off, so the dish itself is not oily at all. Salting the ginger
softens it and speeds up the cooking time. Serve with steamed rice.
If you wish to serve the asparagus as a separate dish, stir-fry them
in 3 tablespoons peanut oil with a little water and with minced garlic
and salt to taste.*

Place the flank steak slices in a bowl and add the soy sauce,
sesame oil and cornstarch. Mix well and let stand at room
temperature for about 30 minutes.

In a separate bowl toss together the ginger and salt and let
stand until the ginger softens, about 20 minutes. Rinse and pat
dry with paper towels.

Warm the peanut oil in a wok or sauté pan over high heat.
Add the beef and fry, separating the slices, for 1–2 minutes.
Using a slotted spoon, transfer the beef to a plate.

Pour off all but 3 tablespoons of the oil. Heat the 3 tablespoons oil over high heat. If using the asparagus, add them
and the water and stir-fry until the water evaporates and the
asparagus are almost cooked, about 2 minutes. Add the ginger,
garlic, if using, beef, wine and sugar. Stir-fry until the beef is
cooked, 1–2 minutes. Serve at once.

Serves 4

Italian Hamburgers or Meatballs alla Pizzaiola

FOR THE SAUCE:

2 tablespoons olive oil

2 teaspoons minced garlic

2 teaspoons dried oregano

1½ cups (12 fl oz/375 ml) basic tomato
  sauce (recipe on page 14)

salt and freshly ground pepper

1½ lb (750 g) ground (minced) beef

⅔ cup (2½ oz/75 g) freshly grated
  Parmesan cheese

2 cups (4 oz/125 g) fresh bread crumbs
  (about 3 slices bread)

1 egg

¼ cup (2 oz/60 g) grated onion

5 tablespoons chopped fresh parsley

3 tablespoons chopped fresh oregano or
  1 tablespoon dried oregano

½ teaspoon freshly ground pepper

¼ cup (2 fl oz/60 ml) olive oil

This ground beef mixture makes great broiled or fried hamburgers or small tasty meatballs. Either spoon the pizzaiola sauce over the cooked burgers or brown the meatballs and then warm them in the sauce. You may, of course, top each patty with fresh mozzarella cheese and then spoon the sauce on top. Serve the burgers on buns or focaccia, and the meatballs with noodles or mashed potatoes.

❧

To prepare the sauce, in a small saucepan warm the oil over low heat. Add the garlic and oregano and sauté until the garlic is soft but not colored, about 4 minutes. Add the tomato sauce and simmer for 5 minutes. Season to taste with salt and pepper.

In a bowl combine the beef, Parmesan, bread crumbs, egg, onion, parsley, oregano and pepper. Using your hands, mix well. Form into 4–6 patties or into meatballs about 1 inch (2.5 cm) in diameter.

Warm the oil in a heavy frying pan over high heat. If making burgers, add to the pan and fry, turning once, until done to your liking. Transfer to individual plates, spoon the sauce over the tops and serve. If making meatballs, add to the pan and fry them beyond medium-rare or they will not hold together. Drain off the excess fat from the pan and add the sauce. Turn the meatballs in the sauce for a few minutes, then serve.

Serves 4–6

Steak au Poivre

5 tablespoons coarsely cracked
  peppercorns
4 slices beef fillet, each about ½ lb (250 g)
  and cut about 1½ inches (4 cm) thick
salt
¼ cup (2 oz/60 g) unsalted butter
1 tablespoon olive oil
½ cup (4 fl oz/125 ml) Cognac or
  Armagnac
½ cup (4 fl oz/125 ml) beef stock
  (*preferably homemade, see page 9*)
2 tablespoons Dijon mustard, optional
1 cup (8 fl oz/250 ml) heavy (double)
  cream

Pepper and steak have a natural affinity. This well-loved classic never goes out of style. It is fast and easy to prepare. Let the pepper-crusted steak sit for about 30 minutes at room temperature before cooking. The optional mustard gives the sauce a distinctive tang. Serve with shoestring potatoes or French fries and green beans or carrots.

Spread the peppercorns on a plate or cutting board. Press the fillets into the cracked peppercorns, turning to coat both sides. Push the peppercorns into the meat with the heel of your hand. Let stand at room temperature for 30 minutes.

Sprinkle the fillets with salt. Combine the butter and oil in a heavy sauté pan or frying pan over high heat. When the pan is hot, add the fillets. Sear, turning once, for 3 minutes per side for rare, or until done to your liking. Transfer to a warmed platter; keep warm.

Pour off the excess fat from the pan. Pour in the Cognac or Armagnac over high heat. Deglaze the pan by stirring to dislodge any browned bits. Add the stock, mustard, if using, and the cream and reduce by half over high heat. Pour over the fillets. Serve at once.

Serves 4

Beef Stroganoff

8 slices beef fillet, each about ½ inch
   (12 mm) thick
freshly ground pepper
6 tablespoons (3 oz/90 g) unsalted butter
2 cups (7 oz/220 g) sliced onions
1 tablespoon sweet Hungarian paprika
2 tablespoons canned tomato purée
5 cups (1 lb/500 g) sliced fresh
   mushrooms
1 cup (8 fl oz/250 ml) beef stock
   (*preferably homemade, see page 9*)
salt
1 tablespoon vegetable oil or olive oil
1 cup (8 fl oz/250 ml) sour cream, at room
   temperature
chopped fresh parsley or dill, optional

In the classic method, the fillet is cut into strips, fried once and then refried in the sauce. This version quickly sears the beef fillet medallions and spoons the Stroganoff sauce on top. The meat will remain juicier and it will look more elegant on the plate. Serve with kasha, fried potatoes or potato pancakes.

*P*lace the fillet slices between 2 sheets of plastic wrap and pound gently with a meat pounder until they are about ¼ inch (6 mm) thick. Season lightly with pepper and set aside.

Melt 2 tablespoons of the butter in a large sauté pan over medium heat. Add the onions and sauté until tender and translucent, about 10 minutes. Stir in the paprika and tomato purée and cook for 1 minute longer. Transfer to a bowl and set aside.

Melt 3 tablespoons of the remaining butter in the same sauté pan over high heat. Add the mushrooms and sauté briefly just until barely tender. Return the onions to the pan, pour in the stock and bring to a simmer. Season to taste with salt and pepper. Remove from the heat and keep warm.

Heat a heavy frying pan over high heat. Add the remaining 1 tablespoon butter and the oil. Add the fillet slices and sear, turning once, about 2 minutes on each side for medium-rare, or until done to your liking.

Divide the fillet slices among 4 plates. Swirl the sour cream into the warm mushroom sauce. Taste and adjust the seasoning and spoon over the cooked fillets. Sprinkle with parsley or dill, if desired.

Serves 4

4 tablespoons (2 oz/60 g) unsalted butter

4 shallots, minced

2 cloves garlic, minced

¼ lb (125 g) fresh mushrooms,
   coarsely chopped

6 fresh sage leaves, finely chopped

24 hazelnuts (filberts), lightly toasted,
   skins removed and chopped
   medium-fine

salt and freshly ground pepper

¼ teaspoon freshly grated nutmeg

1½ lb (750 g) veal scallops, each about
   ⅓ inch (8 mm) thick (12 slices)

6 thin slices prosciutto

3–4 tablespoons (2 fl oz/60 ml) olive oil or
   equal parts olive oil and unsalted butter

1 cup (8 fl oz/250 ml) beef stock
   (*preferably homemade, see page 9*)

1 cup (8 fl oz/250 ml) Marsala

chopped fresh parsley

Veal Rollatini

These little veal rolls may be formed and then refrigerated for up to 12 hours before cooking. To toast and skin hazelnuts, place in a 325°F (165°C) oven until lightly colored, 5–10 minutes. Rub the still-warm nuts in a cotton towel to remove the skins.

Melt 2 tablespoons of the butter in a sauté pan over medium heat. Add the shallots and sauté until softened, about 5 minutes. Add the garlic and mushrooms and cook until most of the mushrooms' liquid evaporates, about 10 minutes. Add the sage and hazelnuts, reserving some of the chopped nuts for garnish, and simmer for 1 minute. Season to taste with salt and pepper and with the nutmeg. Remove from the heat and let cool.

Place the veal scallops between 2 sheets of plastic wrap and pound gently with a meat pounder until they are ¼ inch (6 mm) thick. Cut the prosciutto slices in half and place 1 piece on each piece of veal. Top each with a heaping spoonful of filling. Roll up and tie with kitchen string or skewer closed with wooden toothpicks. Alternatively, thread the rolls on bamboo skewers, putting 2 rolls on each skewer.

Preheat an oven to 350°F (180°C). Heat the oil (or equal parts oil and butter) in a large sauté pan over high heat. Add the rolls and cook, browning on all sides, until tender, 6–8 minutes. Transfer to a baking dish and place in the oven while you make the sauce.

Pour off the excess fat from the pan. Pour in the stock over high heat and deglaze the pan by stirring to dislodge any browned bits. Boil until reduced by half, just a few minutes. Add the Marsala and reduce again by half. Swirl in the remaining 2 tablespoons butter.

Remove the rolls from the oven; discard the skewers or string. Add to the sauce and toss gently. Transfer with the sauce to a platter. Serve at once, topped with parsley and the remaining hazelnuts.

Serves 4

Mexican-Style Skirt Steak

1½–2 lb (750 g–1 kg) skirt steak

FOR THE MARINADE:
1 tablespoon dried oregano
2 tablespoons ground cumin
1 tablespoon chili powder
2 teaspoons finely minced garlic
⅓ cup (3 fl oz/80 ml) beer or red wine
   vinegar

FOR THE SAUCE:
3 tablespoons olive oil
2 large onions, sliced ¼ inch (6 mm) thick
2 green bell peppers (capsicums), seeded,
   deribbed and cut into slices ½ inch
   (12 mm) wide
2 red bell peppers (capsicums), seeded,
   deribbed and cut into slices ½ inch
   (12 mm) wide
2 or 3 fresh jalapeño peppers, seeded, if
   desired, and finely minced
1 tablespoon finely minced garlic
1 tablespoon dried oregano
3 cups (18 oz/560 g) peeled, seeded and
   diced tomatoes, optional
¼ cup (2 fl oz/60 ml) fresh lemon juice
4 tablespoons chopped fresh cilantro
   (fresh coriander)
salt and freshly ground pepper

Skirt steak is a flavorful, chewy cut of meat commonly used for fajitas, *grilled marinated beef strips. It takes to pan-broiling as well: Just smother in this sauce of sautéed onions and peppers, or add the optional tomatoes for a heartier topping. Serve with rice, beans and warm corn tortillas. If you want to temper the fire of the sauce, seed the jalapeño peppers.*

Cut and trim the skirt steak into 4 uniform portions and place in a shallow dish. Some parts of the steak may be thin and some thick, so select the thicker portions for this dish and save the rest for another use.

In a small bowl stir together all the marinade ingredients. Coat the meat with the mixture. Let stand at room temperature for 1–2 hours or cover and refrigerate for 4–6 hours.

Meanwhile, prepare the sauce. Heat the oil in a large sauté pan over medium heat. Add the onions and sauté until softened, 5–7 minutes. Add the green and red peppers and cook for 5–7 minutes longer. Stir in the jalapeños, garlic, oregano and the tomatoes, if using, and cook, stirring, for a few minutes. Add the lemon juice and cilantro; simmer for 1–2 minutes. Taste and adjust the seasoning. Set aside.

Preheat a broiler (griller) or prepare a fire in a charcoal grill. Place the steaks on a rack in a broiler pan and slip under the hot broiler or place on a grill rack over hot coals. Broil or grill, turning once, 3 minutes on each side for rare, or until done to your liking. While the steaks are cooking, reheat the sauce.

Transfer the steaks to a warmed platter and spoon the sauce over the top. Serve at once.

Serves 4

Far Eastern Steak Salad

FOR THE VINAIGRETTE:

2 tablespoons Dijon mustard
3 tablespoons grated fresh ginger
3 tablespoons red wine vinegar
2 tablespoons soy sauce
1 cup (8 fl oz/250 ml) mild olive oil
2 teaspoons brown sugar
salt and freshly ground pepper

1 lb (500 g) flank steak or sirloin steak
salt and freshly ground pepper
½ lb (250 g) green beans, snow peas
   (mangetouts) or snap peas, trimmed
3 bunches watercress or 4 cups (4–5 oz/
   125–155 g) young, tender spinach,
   trimmed and well washed
2 cucumbers, peeled, cut in half
   lengthwise, seeded and cut crosswise
   into slices ⅛ inch (3 mm) thick
2 red bell peppers (capsicums), seeded,
   deribbed and cut into long, thin strips

*Sometimes it pays to cook steak just to have leftovers for salads and
sandwiches. Here is a savory vinaigrette with a Far Eastern accent.*

To prepare the vinaigrette, in a small bowl combine all the
ingredients, including salt and pepper to taste, and whisk until
well blended. Place the steak in a shallow dish. Pour ⅓ cup
(3 fl oz/80 ml) of the vinaigrette over the steak and let stand at
room temperature for about 1 hour.

   Preheat a broiler (griller) until very hot. Sprinkle the steak
with salt and pepper and broil (grill), turning once, 3 minutes
on each side for rare, or until done to your liking. Transfer to
a plate and let cool until it can be handled.

   Bring a saucepan filled with salted water to a boil. Add the
green beans and boil for 4–5 minutes or the snow peas or snap
peas and boil for 2 minutes. Drain immediately and immerse
in ice water until cool. Drain again; pat dry with paper towels.

   Place the watercress or spinach in a bowl, add ¼ cup
(2 fl oz/60 ml) of the vinaigrette and toss well. Divide the
greens among 4 salad plates. In the same bowl combine the
cucumbers, peppers and green beans or peas and ⅓ cup
(3 fl oz/80 ml) of the remaining vinaigrette. Toss well and
divide among the plates. Cut the steak into slices about ¼ inch
(6 mm) thick. Place atop the vegetables. Drizzle the remaining
vinaigrette over the steak.

Serves 4

Korean Grilled Short Ribs

4 lb (2 kg) short ribs

⅓ cup (3 oz/90 g) sugar

½ cup (2 oz/60 g) sesame seeds

¼ cup (2 fl oz/60 ml) Asian sesame oil

½ cup (4 fl oz/125 ml) plus 2 tablespoons
   soy sauce

3 cloves garlic, finely minced

2 teaspoons red pepper flakes

1 tablespoon grated fresh ginger

3 tablespoons all-purpose (plain) flour

While most short ribs are braised or roasted, Korean cooks have an ingenious method of tenderizing the meat before grilling them to a crusty turn. They rub the ribs with sugar to soften the meat and then marinate them in a rich sesame, soy and ginger paste. Steamed rice and garlic-laced spinach crowned with toasted sesame seeds are excellent accompaniments.

Make deep cuts through the meat on the ribs at regular intervals. Rub the sugar into the meat and let stand at room temperature for 30 minutes.

Place the sesame seeds in a small, dry frying pan over medium-low heat and toast, stirring frequently, until golden, about 3 minutes. Let cool, then pulverize using a mortar and pestle.

In a small bowl stir together the ground sesame seeds and all the remaining ingredients. Coat the ribs with the mixture and let stand for about 1 hour longer.

Prepare a fire in a charcoal grill or preheat a broiler (griller) until very hot. Place the ribs on a grill rack over hot coals, or on a rack in a broiler pan and slip under the hot broiler. Grill or broil, turning once, until well browned on the outside but still somewhat rare in the center, about 5 minutes per side, or until done to your liking.

Serves 4 or 5

Broiled Veal Chops alla Valdostana

6 large veal chops, each about ¾ lb (375 g)
    with bone and 1 inch (2.5 cm) thick
6 thin slices prosciutto
6 thin slices Fontina cheese
12 fresh sage leaves
olive oil as needed
salt and freshly ground pepper
2 cups (16 fl oz/500 ml) basic tomato
    sauce, heated (recipe on page 14)

This recipe comes from Val d'Aosta, a mountainous area in the Piedmont region of northern Italy known for its production of Fontina cheese and for its rustic cuisine. The veal chops can be stuffed and refrigerated for 6–8 hours before cooking. The tomato sauce can also be made ahead of time. If you cannot find large, thick veal chops, sandwich thin cutlets together with the filling in the center, dip in seasoned flour, beaten egg and then dried bread crumbs and sauté in butter or olive oil. Top with the sauce. The veal chops or cutlets are delicious served with polenta and broccoli.

Cut a horizontal pocket in each veal chop. Insert 1 prosciutto slice, 1 Fontina cheese slice and 2 sage leaves into each pocket. Alternatively, coarsely chop the prosciutto, cheese and sage, mix together and spread inside each chop pocket.

   Preheat a broiler (griller) until very hot or prepare a fire in a charcoal grill. Brush the chops lightly with oil and sprinkle with salt and pepper. Place the chops on a rack in a broiler pan and slip under the broiler, or place the chops on a grill rack over hot coals. Broil or grill, turning once, about 4 minutes on each side for rare, or until done to your liking. Place on individual plates and spoon the hot tomato sauce over the top.

Serves 6

Latin American Broiled Steak with Avocado Salsa

2 lb (1 kg) flank steak or 4 rib-eye steaks,
   about ½ lb (250 g) each
1 onion, coarsely chopped
2 cloves garlic, finely minced
2 teaspoons ground cumin
2 teaspoons freshly ground pepper
½ cup (4 fl oz/125 ml) fresh lemon juice

FOR THE AVOCADO SALSA:
2 avocados, peeled, pitted and cut into
   ½-inch (12-mm) chunks
4 plum (Roma) tomatoes, peeled, seeded
   and cut into ½-inch (12-mm) chunks
1 teaspoon finely minced fresh jalapeño
   pepper
1 teaspoon finely minced garlic
¼ cup (2 oz/60 g) finely minced green bell
   pepper (capsicum)
3 tablespoons finely minced red (Spanish)
   onion
2 tablespoons red wine vinegar or fresh
   lemon juice
2 tablespoons minced fresh cilantro
   (fresh coriander)
½ cup (4 fl oz/125 ml) olive oil
salt and freshly ground pepper

olive oil as needed
salt

This simple onion and citrus marinade accents the beefiness of the steak. Serve with black beans and tortillas; corn on the cob; or roasted potatoes topped with sour cream and chopped roasted chilies, tomatoes and green (spring) onions.

*P*lace the steak(s) in a shallow dish. Place the onion, garlic, cumin, pepper and lemon juice in a food processor fitted with the metal blade or in a blender and pulse a few times to combine. Pour over the steak(s), cover and let stand for 1 hour at room temperature or cover and refrigerate for 2 hours.

Meanwhile, prepare the salsa. Combine all the ingredients in a bowl and mix well. Set aside at room temperature.

Preheat a broiler (griller) until very hot or prepare a fire in a charcoal grill. Remove the steak(s) from the marinade. Brush lightly with oil and sprinkle with salt. Place on a rack in a broiler pan and slip under the hot broiler, or place on a grill rack over hot coals. Broil or grill, turning once, 3 minutes on each side for rare, or until done to your liking. If preparing flank steak, slice across the grain. Spoon the salsa over the steak and serve.

Serves 4

Broiled Steak with Balsamic Vinegar and Black Pepper

1 sirloin steak, 1½ lb (750 g)
⅓ cup (3 fl oz/80 ml) balsamic vinegar
2 tablespoons olive oil
2 tablespoons honey
1 tablespoon freshly ground pepper
salt

So simple and tasty. Flank steak can stand in for sirloin steak, if you like. Serve with potatoes and broiled mushrooms or radicchio (red chicory) basted with some of the marinade.

*P*lace the steak in a shallow dish. In a small bowl stir together the vinegar, oil, honey and pepper. Pour over the steak. Let stand at room temperature for 1–2 hours.

Preheat a broiler (griller) or prepare a fire in a charcoal grill. Sprinkle the steak lightly with salt. Place the steak on a rack in a broiler pan and slip under the hot broiler, or place the steak on a grill rack over hot coals. Broil or grill, turning once, 3 minutes per side for rare, or until done to your liking. Slice and serve at once.

Serves 4

Beef Kebabs with Pineapple Relish

1½ lb (750 g) beef fillet or sirloin, cut into
    1-inch (2.5-cm) cubes
¼ cup (2 oz/60 g) grated onion
1 tablespoon finely minced garlic
2 tablespoons ground coriander
1 tablespoon ground caraway
2 teaspoons curry powder
2 tablespoons soy sauce
½ cup (4 fl oz/125 ml) coconut milk
2 tablespoons fresh lemon juice

FOR THE PINEAPPLE RELISH:

1 tablespoon peanut oil or vegetable oil
1 onion, thinly sliced
2 fresh red chili peppers, seeded, if
    desired, and chopped
1 small pineapple, peeled and cut into
    1-inch (2.5-cm) cubes
1 teaspoon ground cinnamon
¼ cup (2 oz/60 g) firmly packed
    brown sugar
grated or shredded zest of 1 lemon or
    1 lime
juice of 1 lemon or 2 limes

The marinade used for these kebabs recalls Indonesian satay, except beef cubes rather than thin strips of meat are used here. You can put this same marinade on a whole flank steak. You can also make mango relish by substituting 3 or 4 mangoes, peeled, pitted and cut into ½-inch (12-mm) cubes, for the pineapple. Do not cook the mangoes, however; stir them into the cooled, cooked relish ingredients. Serve the kebabs with steamed rice.

Place the beef in a shallow dish. In a small bowl stir together the onion, garlic, coriander, caraway, curry powder, soy sauce, coconut milk and lemon juice. Pour over the beef and toss to coat on all sides. Let stand at room temperature for 1–2 hours.

Meanwhile, prepare the relish. Heat the oil in a sauté pan over low heat. Add the onion and chilies and sauté until the onion softens, about 5 minutes. Add all the remaining ingredients and cook over medium heat until the pineapple is tender and translucent, about 10 minutes. Remove from the heat, let cool and chill before serving.

Preheat a broiler (griller) or prepare a fire in a charcoal grill. Thread the beef onto skewers. Arrange the skewers on a rack in a broiler pan and slip under the hot broiler, or place the skewers on a grill rack over hot coals. Broil or grill, turning to cook evenly on all sides, 7–8 minutes for medium-rare, or until done to your liking. Serve the kebabs with the relish on the side.

Serves 4

Grilled Steak with Sauce Poivrade

1 onion, finely diced, about 1 cup
 (5 oz/155 g)
1 carrot, finely diced, about ¼ cup
 (1½ oz/45 g)
2 cloves garlic, finely minced
½ cup (4 fl oz/125 ml) red wine vinegar
½ cup (4 fl oz/125 ml) beef stock
 (*preferably homemade, see page 9*)
1 cup (8 fl oz/250 ml) dry red wine
¼ teaspoon ground mace or freshly grated
 nutmeg
1 teaspoon chopped fresh thyme or
 ½ teaspoon dried thyme
1 tablespoon coarsely ground pepper
salt
4 rib-eye steaks, New York strip steaks or
 beef fillet steaks, about ½ lb (250 g)
 each
olive oil as needed
freshly ground pepper
6 tablespoons (3 oz/90 g) unsalted butter
chopped fresh parsley

The traditional French sauce can be prepared a day or so ahead of time, up to the point where the butter is added. Accompany with fried potatoes or potato gratin and some sautéed spinach, which has an affinity for red wine–based sauces.

Combine the onion, carrot, garlic and vinegar in a saucepan over high heat and reduce the liquid by half, just a few minutes. Add the stock, wine, mace or nutmeg and thyme; boil again until reduced by half. Add the coarse pepper and salt to taste and set aside.

 Preheat a broiler (griller) or prepare a fire in a charcoal grill. Brush the steaks with oil and sprinkle lightly with salt and pepper. Place on a rack in a broiler pan and slip under the hot broiler, or place the steaks on a grill rack over hot coals. Broil or grill, turning once, 3 minutes on each side for rare, or until done to your liking. Transfer to a warmed platter.

 Bring the sauce to a boil, reduce the heat and swirl in the butter. Spoon the sauce over the steaks and top with parsley.

Serves 4

Broiled Veal Loin Chops with Tarragon, Mushrooms and Cream

FOR THE SAUCE:

6 tablespoons (3 oz/90 g) unsalted butter
6–8 shallots, diced
¾ lb (375 g) fresh mushrooms, sliced
   ¼ inch (6 mm) thick
2 tablespoons minced fresh tarragon or
   1 tablespoon dried tarragon
½ cup (4 fl oz/125 ml) dry white wine
1 cup (8 fl oz/250 ml) heavy (double)
   cream
salt and freshly ground pepper

6 veal loin chops, each about ¾ lb (375 g)
   with bone
olive oil as needed
salt and freshly ground pepper

Simply broil or grill the chops and top with this rich mushroom-laden tarragon sauce.

Preheat a broiler (griller) until very hot or prepare a fire in a charcoal grill.

To prepare the sauce, melt the butter in a sauté pan over medium heat. Add the shallots and sauté until soft, about 5 minutes. Raise the heat, add the mushrooms and sauté, stirring often, until the mushrooms are tender and give off a little liquid, 1–2 minutes. Add the tarragon, wine and cream and reduce a little. Season to taste with salt and pepper; keep warm.

Brush the veal chops lightly with oil and sprinkle with salt and pepper. Place on a rack in a broiler pan and slip under the hot broiler, or place the chops on a grill rack over hot coals. Broil or grill, turning once, 4 minutes on each side for medium-rare, or until done to your liking. Place the chops on individual plates and spoon the warm sauce over the top.

Serves 6

Oriental Roast Beef

1 whole beef fillet, about 5 lb (2.5 kg)
2 cloves garlic, each cut into 4 slivers
1½ teaspoons salt
½ cup (4 fl oz/125 ml) soy sauce
2 tablespoons grated fresh ginger
2 tablespoons olive oil
1 cup (8 fl oz/250 ml) dry sherry
2 cups (7 oz/220 g) sliced red (Spanish)
    onions
½ cup (4 fl oz/125 ml) beef stock
    (*preferably homemade, see page 9*)

This marinade works equally well on a boneless eye of rib roast, in which case you must omit the oil and double all the remaining marinade ingredients. Serve with a pilaf of long-grain white rice and wild rice, and a stir-fry of snow peas (mangetouts) and shiitake mushrooms.

🌿

*T*rim the beef fillet of all fat and sinews; it should then weigh about 3 lb (1.5 kg). Using the tip of a sharp knife, make 8 slits ½ inch (12 mm) deep at regular intervals in the surface of the fillet. Insert the garlic slivers into the slits. Place in a shallow dish. In a small bowl stir together the salt, soy sauce, ginger, oil and ½ cup (4 fl oz/125 ml) of the sherry. Pour over the meat and turn to coat evenly. Let stand at room temperature for a few hours.

Preheat an oven to 400°F (200°C). Place the onions on the bottom of a roasting pan and place the fillet on top. Roast, basting with a combination of the remaining ½ cup (4 fl oz/ 125 ml) sherry and the beef stock, for 30–40 minutes, or until a meat thermometer reads 115°F (46°C) for very rare, 120°F (49°C) for rare, 125°F (52°C) for medium-rare, or until done to your liking (see page 12).

Transfer the meat to a platter and discard the onions. Let the meat stand for 10 minutes before slicing.

Serves 6

Beer-Basted Prime Rib

8 lb (4 kg) standing rib roast

4–6 cloves garlic, cut into slivers

¼ cup (2 fl oz/60 ml) soy sauce

1 tablespoon freshly ground pepper

½ teaspoon ground allspice

3 cups (24 fl oz/750 ml) dark beer or stout

1 cup (8 fl oz/250 ml) beef stock
   (*preferably homemade, see page 9*)

The beer gives the meat a slightly smoky taste, and deglazing the pan with beef stock and beer provides a rich sauce. Serve with glazed carrots and baked potatoes topped with cold horseradish cream (recipe on page 13) or with mashed potatoes seasoned with freshly grated horseradish. Leftovers make great sandwiches.

🌿

Using the tip of a sharp knife, make slits 1 inch (2.5 cm) deep at regular intervals over the entire surface of the roast. Insert the garlic slivers into the slits. Place in a roasting pan. Brush the outside of the roast with the soy sauce. Sprinkle with the pepper and allspice. Let the roast stand at room temperature for 1 hour.

Preheat an oven to 350°F (180°C). Roast the beef 13 minutes per pound (500 g) or until a meat thermometer reads 120°F (49°C) for rare; 14 minutes per pound or 125°F (52°C) for medium-rare; 15 minutes per pound or 135°F (57°C) for medium; or until done to your liking (see page 12), basting every 10 minutes with dark beer or stout.

Transfer to a warmed platter and let sit for 15 minutes before carving.

Skim the fat from the roasting pan and discard. Place the pan on the stove top over medium-high heat. Pour in the stock (or more beer). Deglaze the pan by stirring to dislodge any browned bits. Simmer a few minutes, then taste and adjust the seasoning. Carve the roast and spoon some of the sauce over the meat.

Serves 6–8

Beef Strudel

3 tablespoons unsalted butter or olive oil,
　plus ½ cup (4 oz/125 g) unsalted butter,
　melted
1 large onion, finely chopped
1 teaspoon minced garlic
3 tablespoons chopped fresh parsley
3 tablespoons chopped fresh dill
1 teaspoon dried oregano
1 teaspoon ground cinnamon
½ teaspoon ground allspice or freshly
　grated nutmeg
1 lb (500 g) ground (minced) beef
1 egg
¼ cup (1 oz/30 g) fine dried bread crumbs
salt and freshly ground pepper
12 sheets filo pastry (about ½ lb)

Sort of a fancy meat loaf, ideal for buffet suppers. Cut on the bias and serve with a dollop of yogurt or sour cream. Steamed or sautéed cucumbers with chives or dill are a nice accompaniment. The strudel can be made up to 12 hours in advance, covered loosely with aluminum foil and refrigerated until baked.

Warm the 3 tablespoons butter or oil in a large frying pan or sauté pan over medium heat. Add the onion and sauté until soft, 8–10 minutes. Add the garlic, parsley, dill, oregano, cinnamon, allspice or nutmeg and beef. Cook until the meat is cooked through, breaking up the beef with a wooden spoon and stirring occasionally, about 10 minutes. Transfer to a bowl and let cool slightly. Stir in the egg and bread crumbs and season to taste with salt and pepper. Let cool for 30 minutes or longer.

Preheat an oven to 350°F (180°C). Butter a baking sheet. Place 1 filo sheet on a clean, dry surface with a long side facing you. Brush with some of the melted butter. Top with a second sheet, brush with more butter and top with a third sheet. Repeat until 6 sheets in all have been used. Place half the meat mixture in a strip along the long edge nearest you, leaving a 1-inch (2.5-cm) border. Fold in the ends and, beginning from the long edge nearest you, roll up like a strudel. Repeat with the remaining sheets and meat mixture to make a second roll.

Place the filo rolls on the prepared baking sheet. Brush with the remaining melted butter. Bake until golden, about 40 minutes. Cut into slices ½ inch (12 mm) thick to serve.

Makes 2 strudels; serves 6

Tomato-Glazed Meat Loaf

2 lb (1 kg) ground (minced) beef chuck

3 slices bread, soaked in tomato juice or milk just to cover and squeezed dry

2 eggs

1 large onion, finely minced

1 tablespoon mixed dried herbs such as sage, oregano and thyme, or 3 tablespoons chopped fresh herbs of choice

4 tablespoons chopped fresh parsley

salt and freshly ground pepper

2 or 3 hard-cooked eggs, optional

1 cup (8 fl oz/250 ml) basic tomato sauce (*recipe on page 14*) or bottled chili sauce

There is nothing quite so comforting as a good meat loaf to remind you of home and happy times. This is a basic, crowd-pleasing meat loaf. If you like, place a row of hard-cooked eggs in the center for a visually exciting slice. Or instead of topping the loaf with tomato sauce or chili sauce, top it with bacon slices and serve with a bowl of warm tomato sauce on the side. Baked or mashed potatoes and a basic green vegetable like peas are good accompaniments. And don't forget wonderful meat loaf sandwiches with a little chili sauce rubbed on the bread.

🌿

Preheat an oven to 350°F (180°C). Grease a baking pan.

In a bowl combine the meat, bread, eggs, onion, herbs, parsley and salt and pepper to taste. Mix well with your hands. Form the meat mixture into an oval loaf. If you like, place the hard-cooked eggs in a row down the center of the loaf as you form it. Place the loaf in the pan and pour the tomato or chili sauce over the top.

Bake until cooked through, about 1¼ hours. Let stand for 15 minutes, then slice and serve.

Serves 4

Rib-Eye Roast with Mustard, Ginger and Lemon

1 boneless rib-eye roast, about 4 lb (2 kg)
6 cloves garlic, cut into slivers
½ cup (4 oz/125 g) sliced, peeled fresh
   ginger
½ cup (4 fl oz/125 ml) fresh lemon juice
1 cup (8 oz/250 g) Dijon mustard
1 teaspoon freshly ground pepper

A Far Eastern accent to an all-American roast. An 8-pound (4-kg) standing rib roast can replace the boneless rib eye. Serve with stir-fried asparagus and carrots, and rice pilaf tossed with pistachios and currants.

🌿

Using the tip of a sharp knife, make slits 1 inch (2.5 cm) deep at regular intervals over the entire surface of the meat. Insert one-third of the garlic slivers into the slits. Place the remaining garlic and the ginger in a blender or in a food processor fitted with the metal blade. Process to a paste, adding some of the lemon juice as needed to moisten the ginger. Add the mustard, the remaining lemon juice and the pepper and process to mix well. Alternatively, combine the ingredients in a bowl and beat together with a wooden spoon, or combine them in a mortar and pound them together with a pestle.

Coat the roast with the mustard mixture, place in a roasting pan (on a rack, if you like) and let stand at room temperature for about 2 hours.

Preheat an oven to 350°F (180°C). Roast the beef 13 minutes per pound (500 g) or until a meat thermometer reads 120°F (49°C) for rare; 14 minutes per pound or 125°F (52°C) for medium-rare; 15 minutes per pound or 135°F (57°C) for medium; or until done to your liking (see page 12). Let stand for 15 minutes before carving.

Serves 6–8